ESP teaching and teacher education: current theories and practices

Edited by Salomi Papadima-Sophocleous,
Elis Kakoulli Constantinou,
and Christina Nicole Giannikas

Published by Research-publishing.net, a not-for-profit association
Voillans, France, info@research-publishing.net

© 2019 by Editors (collective work)
© 2019 by Authors (individual work)

ESP teaching and teacher education: current theories and practices
Edited by Salomi Papadima-Sophocleous, Elis Kakoulli Constantinou, and Christina Nicole Giannikas

Publication date: 2019/06/22

Rights: the whole volume is published under the Attribution-NonCommercial-NoDerivatives International (CC BY-NC-ND) licence; **individual articles may have a different licence**. Under the CC BY-NC-ND licence, the volume is freely available online (https://doi.org/10.14705/rpnet.2019.33.9782490057450) for anybody to read, download, copy, and redistribute provided that the author(s), editorial team, and publisher are properly cited. Commercial use and derivative works are, however, not permitted.

Disclaimer: Research-publishing.net does not take any responsibility for the content of the pages written by the authors of this book. The authors have recognised that the work described was not published before, or that it was not under consideration for publication elsewhere. While the information in this book is believed to be true and accurate on the date of its going to press, neither the editorial team nor the publisher can accept any legal responsibility for any errors or omissions. The publisher makes no warranty, expressed or implied, with respect to the material contained herein. While Research-publishing.net is committed to publishing works of integrity, the words are the authors' alone.

Trademark notice: product or corporate names may be trademarks or registered trademarks, and are used only for identification and explanation without intent to infringe.

Copyrighted material: every effort has been made by the editorial team to trace copyright holders and to obtain their permission for the use of copyrighted material in this book. In the event of errors or omissions, please notify the publisher of any corrections that will need to be incorporated in future editions of this book.

Typeset by Research-publishing.net
Cover layout by © 2019 Raphaël Savina (raphael@savina.net)

ISBN13: 978-2-490057-45-0 (Ebook, PDF, colour)
ISBN13: 978-2-490057-46-7 (Ebook, EPUB, colour)
ISBN13: 978-2-490057-44-3 (Paperback - Print on demand, black and white)
Print on demand technology is a high-quality, innovative and ecological printing method; with which the book is never 'out of stock' or 'out of print'.

British Library Cataloguing-in-Publication Data.
A cataloguing record for this book is available from the British Library.

Legal deposit, UK: British Library.
Legal deposit, France: Bibliothèque Nationale de France - Dépôt légal: juin 2019.

Table of contents

v   Acknowledgements

1   Introduction
Salomi Papadima-Sophocleous, Elis Kakoulli Constantinou, and Christina Nicole Giannikas

13   ESP in teacher education: a case study
Yasemin Kırkgöz

27   Finding the way through the ESP maze: designing an ESP teacher education programme
Elis Kakoulli Constantinou, Salomi Papadima-Sophocleous, and Nicos Souleles

47   Self-scaffolding and the role of new technologies in ESP teacher education
Irena Aleksić-Hajduković, Danka Sinadinović, and Stevan Mijomanović

63   Providing feedback on the lexical use of ESP students' academic presentations: teacher training considerations
Alla Zareva

79   Validating new perspectives and methodologies for learning and teacher training in English for aeronautical communications
Neil Bullock

95   Technology-enhanced curriculum development in the ESP tertiary context
Christina Nicole Giannikas

111   Embedding a serious game into an ESP curriculum
Giouli Pappa and Salomi Papadima-Sophocleous

131   Facilitating the development of collaborative online dictionaries in the ESP field
Eleni Nikiforou

Table of contents

147 Going beyond words and actions: teaching metacognitive and soft skills to ESP communication students at the dawn of the fourth industrial revolution
Dana Di Pardo Léon-Henri

163 Pronunciation instruction in ESP teaching to enhance students' prosody
Leticia Quesada Vázquez

177 Author index

Acknowledgements

The editors of *ESP teaching and teacher education: current theories and practices* would like to wholeheartedly thank the Language Centre of the Cyprus University of Technology for its support in the publication of this volume.

Salomi Papadima-Sophocleous,
Elis Kakoulli Constantinou,
and Christina Nicole Giannikas

Introduction

Salomi Papadima-Sophocleous[1], Elis Kakoulli Constantinou[2], and Christina Nicole Giannikas[3]

As the demand for more highly skilled and qualified 21st century professionals is increasing, and vast amounts of populations are moving from one place to another worldwide, the numbers of English for Specific Purposes (ESP) courses are constantly growing. Learners nowadays need courses to cater for their needs dictated by the demands of the labour market (Jendrych, 2013). In this ever changing context, ESP has started to receive much attention by teachers, learners, and researchers in the field; as a result, there has been an increase in the organisation of conferences and colloquia and the creation of professional organisations related to ESP. Despite the developments in ESP research and practice, however, the literature shows that there are areas of ESP that remain pristine and unexplored.

Researchers in the field admit that studies on issues pertaining to ESP mainly focus on text or discourse analysis (Hewings, 2002), genre, and corpus studies (Johns, 2013) or on the analysis of the learners' needs. Basturkmen (2012) supports that Language for Specific Purposes (LSP) research in general "has been overly concerned with planning what should be taught, to the relative neglect of inquiry into implementation of LSP and issues related to teaching" (p. 60).

Issues related to ESP teacher education have not been thoroughly investigated yet. Publications focussing on ESP teacher education are very few, and they

---

1. Cyprus University of Technology, Limassol, Cyprus; salomi.papadima@cut.ac.cy; https://orcid.org/0000-0003-4444-4482

2. Cyprus University of Technology, Limassol, Cyprus; elis.constantinou@cut.ac.cy; https://orcid.org/0000-0001-8854-3816

3. Cyprus University of Technology, Limassol, Cyprus; christina.giannikas@cut.ac.cy; https://orcid.org/0000-0002-5653-6803

How to cite: Papadima-Sophocleous, S., Kakoulli Constantinou, E., & Giannikas, C. N. (2019). Introduction. In S. Papadima-Sophocleous, E. Kakoulli Constantinou & C. N. Giannikas (Eds), *ESP teaching and teacher education: current theories and practices* (pp. 1-12). Research-publishing.net. https://doi.org/10.14705/rpnet.2019.33.922

mostly involve journal articles. Books or edited volumes on ESP teacher education are hard to find, and apart from Howard and Brown's (1997) volume entitled *Teacher Education for LSP*, there has not been any other endeavour to publish a volume dedicated to this issue. In all the publications focussing on ESP teacher education, the view which unanimously prevails is the one that expresses the need for more opportunities for ESP teacher training and thus more research in this field (Abdulaziz, Shah, Mahmood, & Fazal e Haq, 2012; Adnan, 2011; Bezukladnikov & Kruze, 2012; Bojović, 2006; Bracaj, 2014; Chen, 2012; Fortanet-Gomez & Räisänen, 2008; Howard, 1997; Johnstone, 1997; Kakoulli Constantinou & Papadima-Sophocleous, 2017; Kennedy, 1983; Madhavi Latha, 2014; Mahapatra, 2011; Master, 1997; Mebitil, 2011; Rajabi, Kiany, & Maftoon, 2012; Savas, 2009; Wright, 2012; Zavasnik, 2007).

Apart from issues related to ESP teacher education, another area that has not received enough attention is that of ESP teaching methodology and the use of new technologies, although its value has been continuously expressed in literature (Blake, 2013; Donaldson & Haggstorm, 2006; Hanson-Smith, 1999; Walker & White, 2013). As Basturkmen (2014) claims, there have been only a few empirical studies investigating the work of ESP teachers and LSP teachers in general.

The limited research in the areas of ESP teacher education and ESP teaching, including the use of new technologies, and the intense need for ESP teacher training that have been detected in the ESP literature are the sources of inspiration for this proposed volume. Another factor that is considered as an impetus behind this publication is the belief that ESP is still a field that is advancing, and this can be proven by the ongoing evolvement of ESP, which "has been changing and developing all the time, and it is expected to change and develop in the future as well" (Jendrych, 2013, p. 43). The various socio-economic and demographic changes occurring worldwide created the demand for more capable professionals who are able to communicate effectively in their professional environment. In such a context, the need for more efficient ESP teaching practices and more proficient and research-based ESP teacher training is nowadays more powerful than ever.

The purpose of this edited volume, supported by the Language Centre of the Cyprus University of Technology, is to give the opportunity to researchers and practitioners to share their knowledge, skills, and experiences in ESP teaching and teacher education and trigger further interest in this domain. The aim is to further explore and share ESP research and practices.

The volume consists of an introduction, ten chapters, and bio statements for editors. It aims at addressing issues related to ESP teacher education and ESP teaching practices as they arise in today's constantly changing and developing world. It puts together a selection of chapters on issues pertaining to ESP teacher education and ESP teaching methodology.

The first five chapters focus on different aspects of ESP teacher education, including that of the use of new technologies.

In chapter one, entitled *ESP in teacher education: a case study*, **Kırkgöz** addresses the professional needs of future ESP teachers by designing an innovative ESP teacher education course in a teacher education programme in Turkey. The theoretical framework of the study is based on the constructivist perspective in order to help pre-service English teachers create meaning through their participation in various socialisation practices. The first part of the course was theory-informed to familiarise students with ESP-related topics, while the second part followed a practice-oriented approach. Data were collected through pre- and post-test open-ended questionnaires, student journals, and ESP projects. Content analysis was used to analyse the qualitative data. Findings underline the positive effects of the ESP course. Suggestions are offered for teacher education programmes.

In chapter two, entitled *Finding the way through the ESP maze: designing an ESP teacher education programme*, **Kakoulli Constantinou**, **Papadima-Sophocleous**, and **Souleles** report on the first findings of a technical action research study, which aims at exploring and addressing the problem of insufficient ESP teacher education suggesting an intervention in the form of an online ESP teacher education programme. Following the spiral pattern of action research, the study evolves in cycles of continuous improvement. The chapter focusses on the initial stages of the study, during which the problem of lack of ESP teacher education opportunities was identified, and a remedy to this problem, an online ESP teacher education course, named Online Reflective Teacher Education in ESP (ReTEESP Online), was developed and piloted with a group of ESP practitioners before its implementation.

In chapter three, entitled *Self-scaffolding and the role of new technologies in esp teacher education,* **Aleksić-Hajduković**, **Sinadinović**, and **Mijomanović** explore how ESP teachers and practitioners utilise new technologies, e.g. massive open online courses, webinars, online platforms, etc. as a means of self-scaffolding in order to exceed their threshold in pedagogical, linguistic, and discoursal competencies in various ESP domains. The study analyses the data provided by ESP teachers and practitioners from various educational backgrounds. The findings obtained via a questionnaire show to what extent ESP teachers and practitioners exploit new technologies as a means of self-scaffolding, but also offer a classification of the tools, strategies, and opportunities available for their self-directed unassisted professional development. Furthermore, various electronic self-scaffolding resources are discussed and evaluated according to their accessibility, applicability, and popularity among teachers. While this research is not concerned with cross-cultural differences in ESP teacher education, broadly speaking, it is concerned with gathering data from various teaching environments with a view to providing a universal representation of current trends in ESP teacher education. Offering an up-to-date model for ESP teacher education is an important implication of this research and the authors hope its findings serve as guidelines and contribute to material development.

In chapter four, entitled *Providing feedback on the lexical use of ESP students' academic presentations: teacher training considerations,* **Zareva** describes a methodology for providing training to pre-service EAP/ESP teacher trainees in giving evidence-based feedback on the lexical composition of ESP students' academic presentations. The author discusses a study based on the analysis of the mock feedback provided by the EAP/ESP teacher trainees to ESP students' presentations with a focus on the effects of training. The results reveal that the training was successful in areas such as raising the teacher trainees' awareness of how to evaluate various lexical categories in an ESP presentation, how to incorporate their evaluation into the feedback they give to the students, how to highlight relevant lexical deviations in an evidence-based manner, etc. but there were also a couple of areas that needed to be emphasised more in the training process. The results confirmed that providing training on evidence-driven feedback to teacher trainees planning to teach in an EAP/ESP context is a necessary component of ESP teacher education.

In chapter five, entitled *Context & communication in ESP – validating new perspectives and methodologies for learners and teacher training in English for aeronautical communication,* and based on evidence from research conducted in previous years, **Bullock** conducted classroom-based research with 33 air traffic controller students, undergoing their basic operational and technical training at the ROMATSA training centre in Constanta, Romania. That earlier research argued for a change of perspectives in LSP teaching and for a more appropriate and valid methodology for English learners in the aeronautical domain by adopting a more inclusive communication and knowledge-based approach in order to fill the disconnect between what is often taught and what is used in the real world. The aim was to demonstrate how the transfer of such theory into practice would address real world communication needs. The chapter gives supporting background evidence to the research, followed by the rationale and methods used in the research. It demonstrates the positive impact such methodology had on the students and their learning and suggests more appropriate training and education for LSP teachers, which would offer learners the most appropriate environment in which to maintain and improve their communication skills through language.

The next five chapters focus on ESP teaching with the use of technologies.

In chapter six, entitled *Technology-enhanced curriculum development in a coursebook-based learning culture: the ESP tertiary context,* **Giannikas** focusses on a curriculum that was developed to tailor the academic and professional needs of 20 ESP first year students of the Department of Chemical

Engineering, with the aid of a technology-enhanced environment. The aim of the personalised curriculum was to stress the fusion of interactive tools and make use of applications that would deliver opportunities for: (1) autonomy, (2) resource and content management, and (3) communal and individual content production, presentation, and sharing. Data reports on the transformational period, the progress made, and the impact the technology-enhanced curriculum had on their learning. The investigation revealed insights on the level of intensity of cognitive and instrumental interactivity.

In chapter seven, entitled *Embedding a serious game into ESP curriculum*, **Pappa** and **Papadima-Sophocleous** describe how a selected Commercial Off-the-shelf (COTS) Serious Game (SG) was evaluated before being integrated into ESP curriculum through the steps and decisions taken before the implementation of the selected COTS SG in a specific ESP learning context. The aim of the single-case study was to explore the areas of ESP teaching with COTS SGs, by illustrating a combination of assessment methods that could be adopted by those considering embedding SG in formal ESP language settings. First, the authors outline the reasons which initiated such an integration. Then, they present the validation of their selection process of the particular SG through an initial assessment of the game and the game design. After evaluating its pedagogical use, they analyse the way they considered applying the selected tool within the curriculum.

In chapter eight, entitled *Facilitating the development of collaborative online dictionaries in the ESP field*, **Nikiforou** reports on the results of data taken from a course in a tertiary institution in Cyprus. English Foreign Language (EFL) students worked collaboratively on a wiki to complete the task of creating a shared online biomedical dictionary. The methodology that lies behind the research is grounded theory. The research conducted is qualitative and as such the data are primarily collected from the wiki and the history pages which kept track of the students' work. Emphasis is given both on the frequency with which the students entered the wiki to add, edit, and format vocabulary items, and the quality of their vocabulary entries, including the editing of the items that followed. This chapter offers practical suggestions on how to design and implement such a task in any ESP and EFL course across different language levels as well as in mixed ability classrooms.

In chapter nine, entitled *Going beyond words and actions: teaching metacognitive and soft skills to ESP communication students at the dawn of the fourth industrial revolution,* **Di Pardo Léon-Henri** examines ways in which new technologies can be integrated into reflective ESP teaching methods to stimulate student motivation and encourage the development of the aforementioned skills which are not only professional but also metacognitive in nature, within the context of non-specialist English language students in communication studies. The chapter begins by presenting the theoretical framework, method, and procedures for a collaborative one-minute film project. Finally, it presents some initial results, as well as various observations and potential for further transversal research.

In chapter ten, entitled *Pronunciation instruction in ESP teaching to enhance students' prosody,* **Quesada Vázquez** investigates the efficacy of explicit rhythm instruction to improve engineering students' prosody in English. As part of this research project, a pronunciation module, consisting of ten weekly sessions of 30 minutes held within the class schedule, was designed for a technical English course at Rovira I Virgili University. According to the author, every session followed Celce-Murcia's steps to teach communicatively. The participants were 298 Spanish/Catalan first year undergraduates divided into three experimental and three control groups. Experimental groups received explicit rhythm instruction while control groups did not. All students were recorded before and after the training. Six native American English speakers were also recorded as a reference point. Varco-V values were calculated and compared using Praat and the data were analysed using mixed analysis of variances and t-tests. Results reveal that students who took rhythm instruction tend to increase in Varco-V after training, approaching English rhythm, while those who did not train rhythm present broader variance. Despite results not always being significant, an analysis of the effect sizes for the t-tests comparing before and after Varco-V values for the experimental versus the control groups show significance. These results, though preliminary, support the hypothesis that rhythm instruction can be beneficial to improve ESP students' prosody.

Introduction

The audience for this volume is expected to be a broad one, since the issues on which it focusses may be of interest to many specialists in the field. More specifically, it is expected that this volume will appeal to ESP teacher trainers or language teacher trainers in general, who would like to learn about the newest research, ideas, and practices in the field of ESP teacher training. The volume will also attract the interest of ESP practitioners who wish to be informed about the latest developments in the field of ESP teaching and the opportunities that they may have for professional development in the field. Moreover, the volume may also be useful to ESP researchers, teacher trainers, practitioners, policymakers, material developers, students, as well as any other ESP specialists who may be interested in being updated about the latest developments in the ESP field.

References

Abdulaziz, M., Shah, S. K., Mahmood, R., & Fazal e Haq, H. M. (2012). Change from a general English teacher to an ESP practitioner: issues and challenges in Pakistan. *Interdisciplinary Journal of Contemporary Research in Business, 4*(1), 434-465.

Adnan, S. (2011). The important skills ESP teachers need to be qualified to teach ESP courses. *Basra Studies Journal, 11*(11), 45-67.

Basturkmen, H. (2012). Languages for specific purposes curriculum creation and implementation in Australasia and Europe. *The Modern Language Journal, 96*(1), 59-70. https://doi.org/10.1111/j.1540-4781.2012.01297.x

Basturkmen, H. (2014). LSP teacher education: review of literature and suggestions for the research agenda. *Iberica, 28*, 17-34.

Bezukladnikov, K., & Kruze, B. (2012). An outline of an ESP teacher training course. *World Applied Sciences Journal, 20* (Special Issue of Pedagogy and Psychology), 103-106.

Blake, R. J. (2013). *Brave new digital classroom: technology and foreign language learning* (2nd ed.). Georgetown University Press.

Bojović, M. (2006). Teaching foreign language for specific purposes: teacher development. In M. Brejc (Ed.), *Co-operative partnerships in teacher education proceedings of the 31st Annual ATEE Conference, Slovenia.* (pp. 1-3). National School for Leadership in Education. http://www.pef.uni-lj.si/atee/

Bracaj, M. (2014). Teaching English for specific purposes and teacher training. *European Scientific Journal, 10*(2), 40-49.

Chen, Y. (2012). ESP development in Taiwan: an overview. *ESP News, TESOL International Association.* http://newsmanager.commpartners.com/tesolespis/issues/2012-08-21/2.html

Donaldson, R. P., & Haggstorm, M. A. (2006). *Changing language education through CALL.* Routledge.

Fortanet-Gomez, I., & Räisänen, C. A. (2008). The state of ESP teaching and learning in Western European higher education after Bologna. In I. Fortanet-Gomez & C. A. Räisänen (Eds), *ESP in European higher education: integrating language and content* (pp. 11-50). John Benjamins Publishing. https://doi.org/10.1075/aals.4.03rai

Hanson-Smith, E. (1999). CALL environments. The quiet revolution. *ESL Magazine, 2*(2), 8-12.

Hewings, M. (2002). A history of ESP through English for specific purposes. *English for Specific Purposes World, 3*(1). http://www.esp-world.info/Articles_3/Hewings_paper_Bio.htm

Howard, R. (1997). LSP in the UK. In R. Howard & G. Brown (Eds), *Teacher education for LSP* (pp. 55-57). Multilingual Matters.

Howard, R., & Brown, G. (Eds). (1997). *Teacher education for languages for specific purposes.* Multilingual Matters Ltd.

Jendrych, E. (2013). Developments in ESP teaching. *Studies in Logic, Grammar and Rhetoric, 34*(1), 43-58. https://doi.org/10.2478/slgr-2013-0022

Johns, A. M. (2013). The history of English for specific purposes research. In B. Paltridge & S. Starfield (Eds), *The handbook of English for specific purposes* (pp. 5-30). John Wiley & Sons, Inc. https://doi.org/10.1002/9781118339855.ch1

Johnstone, R. (1997). LSP teacher education (foreign languages): common and specific elements. In R. Howard & G. Brown (Eds), *Teacher education for LSP* (pp. 11-21). Multilingual Matters.

Kakoulli Constantinou, E., & Papadima-Sophocleous, S. (2017). ESP teacher education: an online, in-service, ESP teacher training course. In T. Pattison (Ed.), *IATEFL 2016 Birmingham Conference Selections.* 50th International Conference, Birmingham, 13-16 April 2016, Kent: Pilgrims.

Kennedy, C. (1983). An ESP approach to EFL/ESL teacher training. *ESP Journal, 2*(1), 73-85. https://doi.org/10.1016/0272-2380(83)90024-0

Madhavi Latha, B. (2014). Teacher education and ESP. *IMPACT: International Journal of Research in Humanities, Arts and Literature, 2*(4), 73-82.

Mahapatra, S. K. (2011). Teacher training in ESP: a historical review. *English for Specific Purposes World, 11*(33), 1-15.

Master, P. (1997). ESP teacher education in the USA. In R. Howard & G. Brown (Eds), *Teacher education for LSP* (pp. 22-40). Multilingual Matters.

Mebitil, N. (2011). *An exploration of the main difficulties, challenges and requirements of the ESP teaching situation in Algeria: the case of ESP teachers at Abou Bekr Belkaid University, Tlemcen.* Abou Bekr Belkaid University – Tlemcen. http://dspace.univ-tlemcen.dz/bitstream/112/317/1/AN-EXPLORATION-OF-THE-MAIN-DIFFICULTIES-CHALLENGES-AND-REQUIREMENTS-OF-THE-ESP-TEACHING-SITUATION-IN-ALGERIA.THE-CASE-OF-ESP-TEACHERS-AT-ABOUBEKR-BELKAID.pdf

Rajabi, P., Kiany, G. R., & Maftoon, P. (2012). ESP in-service teacher training programs: do they change Iranian teachers' beliefs, classroom practices and students' achievements? *Iberica, 24,* 261-282.

Savas, B. (2009). Role of functional academic literacy in ESP teaching: ESP teacher training in Turkey for sustainable development. *The Journal of International Social Research, 2*(9), 395-406.

Walker, A., & White, G. (2013). *Technology enhanced language learning: connecting theory and practice.* Oxford University Press.

Wright, R. (2012). Throwing CELTA grads an ESP lifeline. *ESP News, The Newsletter of the English for Specific Purposes Interest Section, TESOL International Association,* (December). http://newsmanager.commpartners.com/tesolespis/issues/2012-12-18/8.html

Zavasnik, M. (2007). ESP teacher training needs: the case of Slovenia. In *XVI Symposium on Language for Special Purposes (LSP) Book of Abstracts: Specialised Language in Global Communication* (pp. 97-98). University of Hamburg. https://nats-www.informatik.uni-hamburg.de/pub/LSP07/Section2Tue/Zavasnik.pdf

About the editors

Salomi Papadima-Sophocleous (Chief-Editor) holds a doctorate in applied linguistics. She is the Cyprus University of Technology Language Centre Director, its online MA in CALL Coordinator, and a language teacher trainer for the University of Cyprus Education Department. She is currently a EUROCALL Association Executive Committee member and the Association Nine SIGs' coordinator. Her research interests are in the field of Applied Linguistics, focussing on CALL, computer assisted language assessment and testing, ESP, teacher education, and curriculum development. She is the editor of *The ALCUIN teacher guide to motivating students to read literature* (2010), and the co-editor of *International experiences in language testing and assessment* (2013), *CALL communities and culture* (2016), and *Professional development in CALL: a selection of papers* (2019). She is also the author of teaching material: *Geia sou* (1995), *Greek! Why not?* (2001), *Voilà 1 & 2* (2002), co-author of *Ça alors! 1 & 2* (1998, 2002), and the designer and developer of the New English Placement Test Online (NEPTON) (2005). Moreover, she has a special interest in oral history. She is the editor of a series of annual volumes on Limassol Oral History since 2007.

Elis Kakoulli Constantinou holds an MA in applied linguistics, and she is currently a PhD candidate in the area of ESP teacher education. She is an ESP instructor at the Cyprus University of Technology Language Centre and a teacher trainer at the Cyprus Pedagogical Institute of the Cyprus Ministry of Education and Culture. Her research interests revolve around English for Specific Purposes (ESP), ESP teacher education, English language curriculum development, the latest developments in language teaching methods, and the integration of new technologies in language teaching. Her work has been published in peer-reviewed journals and volumes and has been presented in a number of academic conferences. She is a co-editor of the EuroCALL Teacher Education SIG volume *Professional development in CALL: a selection of papers* (2019), and she is also a member of various professional organisations.

Christina Nicole Giannikas holds a PhD in the field of applied linguistics. She is Chair of the EuroCALL Teacher Education Special Interest Group (SIG) and Chief Editor of the Teacher Education SIG's recent edited volume *Professional development in CALL: a selection of papers*. She currently works for the Language Centre at Cyprus University of Technology and is a pre-service teacher trainer for the Education Department of the University of Cyprus. Christina has taught courses in teaching methods in EFL, second language acquisition, research methodologies, understanding the language classroom, as well as ESP

Introduction

in chemical engineering, nursing, and shipping in higher education. She has been involved in a number of research projects with a focus on computer assisted language learning in early language learning contexts, digital storytelling, and literacy, student-centred teaching approaches, language teaching policies, teacher education, and professional development, language assessment literacy, special education in the primary school context, and e-learning/blended learning in higher education.

1 ESP in teacher education: a case study

Yasemin Kırkgöz[1]

Abstract

The growing importance of global English has led to the rise of English for Specific Purposes (ESP) teaching, particularly in higher education. Despite the concurrently increasing demand for ESP teachers, pre-service teacher education programmes have largely neglected this important area. This study has been initiated to address the professional needs of future ESP teachers by designing an innovative ESP teacher education course in a teacher education programme in Turkey. The theoretical framework of the study is based on the constructivist perspective in order to help pre-service English teachers create meaning through their participation in various socialisation practices. The first part of the course was theory-informed to familiarise students with ESP-related topics, while the second part followed a practice-oriented approach. Data were collected through pre-and post-test open-ended questionnaires, student journals, and ESP projects. Content analysis was used to analyse the qualitative data. Findings underline the positive effects of the ESP course. Suggestions are offered for teacher education programmes.

Keywords: constructivism, English for specific purposes, pre-service teachers, teacher education.

---

1. Çukurova University, Adana, Turkey; ykirkgoz@gmail.com; https://orcid.org/0000-0001-5838-6637

How to cite this chapter: Kırkgöz, Y. (2019). ESP in teacher education: a case study. In S. Papadima-Sophocleous, E. Kakoulli Constantinou & C. N. Giannikas (Eds), *ESP teaching and teacher education: current theories and practices* (pp. 13-26). Research-publishing.net. https://doi.org/10.14705/rpnet.2019.33.923

Chapter 1

1. Introduction

With the effects of globalisation and an increase in the demand for qualified professionals in the 21st century, teaching ESP has started to draw greater attention. Currently, learners need courses to cater for their specific needs to serve the demands of the society. As a result, ESP has started to attract growing attention from policy-makers, course designers, teachers, and learners. Despite its growing importance, the field of ESP remains an unexplored territory in teacher education (Basturkmen, 2017). Teacher education programs in Turkey and many other countries do not always prepare prospective teachers with the essential knowledge and skills of how to teach learners with specific needs and purposes. It is acknowledged that unlike teaching English for general purposes, teaching ESP is demanding as it includes a range of tasks: identifying learner needs, developing courses and materials, as well as classroom teaching (Basturkmen, 2014; Hutchinson & Waters, 1987). Therefore, practising ESP teachers often require additional knowledge and skills.

The majority of studies in the ESP literature concern needs analysis, course design, materials development, and training practising teachers (Basturkmen, 2010; Belcher, 2006). However, little is known about how to prepare pre-service teachers for ESP professions (Hyslop-Margison & Strobel, 2007). This study aims to contribute to the literature by designing an ESP teacher education course in a teacher education programme in Turkey. After providing a theoretical perspective on constructivism, the methodology section presents the framework of the ESP course, participants, data collection, and data analysis. This is followed by a presentation and discussion of the research findings.

The epistemological foundations of constructivism and the theory's implications for classroom practice are laid down by Lev Vygotsky (1978) and John Dewey (1929). Vygotsky's (1978) theory of knowledge acquisition espouses the view that knowledge is socially negotiated in cooperation with others and that individual cognition acts as the generating force in knowledge construction. In a constructivist perspective, the learner is recognised as an active participant with prior knowledge and experience, which determines how new learning can be assimilated or accommodated (Hughes & Sears, 2004).

In the social constructivist pedagogy, the instructor holds a pivotal figure in the classroom through modelling and guided instruction. The instructor creates activities that help students adjust their conceptual understanding to advance beyond their present level of development to a higher level within the conceptual distance – the Zone of Proximal Development (ZPD) (Hyslop-Margison & Sears, 2006). In the context of ZPD, Vygotsky (1978) emphasised the vital role of imitation. As learners imitate teachers by watching demonstrations and responding to questions, they learn new ideas which exceed their present level of knowledge (Smith, 2001). Besides, in a constructivist classroom, teachers and students are regarded as co-constructors of meaningful interactions, and lecturing is seen as a pedagogically acceptable and valuable instructional tool when used in the proper context.

Dewey (1929) postulated that direct experience is key to learning in children who must start with direct, concrete real-life experiences to help connect learning to their world. Likewise, Smith (2001) noted that "novices of any age and of any subject matter benefit from direct [...] experience, [noting that] this can be effective if it includes ongoing, adequate, and focused guidance by a more experienced peer or teacher educator" (p. 223). The constructivist epistemologies of Dewey (1929) and Vygotsky (1978) offer useful implications in improving our understanding of the kind of experiences ESP teacher candidates confront when learning new knowledge, and they also offer useful pedagogical strategies for its classroom application in an ESP teacher education course.

2. Method

Situated within the constructivist paradigm, and using mainly qualitative inquiry as a research approach (Creswell, 2013), the study sought answers to the following research questions.

- How do the Turkish pre-service English language teachers perceive ESP and ESP-related issues prior to the ESP teacher education course?

- How do the Turkish pre-service English language teachers perceive ESP and ESP-related issues after participating in the ESP teacher education course?

- To what extent do the Turkish pre-service English language teachers feel prepared to teach ESP in their future profession?

2.1. Data collection and analysis

To address the above-listed research questions, data were collected from 60 pre-service teacher candidates enrolled in the ESP course offered in the spring semester in the third-year of the teacher education programme. Data collection tools included a pre-and post-ESP questionnaire which contained ten open-ended items administered both at the beginning and at the end of the 14-week course, reflective journals which participants wrote weekly, and participants' ESP projects. The qualitative data were subjected to content analysis.

Data from the pre-ESP questionnaire were examined to determine participants' responses to each question, and the post-ESP questionnaire was examined to decide on the degree of change, if any, in the students' responses to each questionnaire item. Qualitative data from the reflective journals were coded and analysed for patterns and themes corresponding to each research question (Creswell, 2013). The participants' written reflections on their ESP learning experience were used to support the emerging themes found in the questionnaire data, and ESP projects were used for illustrative purposes. Information from each student was recorded under a separate file, using a *pseudonym f*or each participant such as Özge, Arda, Cem, Onur, Seval, Erdem, Salih, Kaan, İpek, and Mutlu.

2.2. Conceptual framework of the ESP course

The ESP course was comprised of two main components. The first part of the course (Weeks 1-7) involved imparting knowledge through lecturing, complemented with small group or pair-work tasks. In line with Dewey's (1929) model of constructivism which situates the instructor as a classroom facilitator and Vygotsky's (1978) idea of modelling as relational initiation (Smith, 2001), students were assisted to construct epistemological knowledge of basic ESP concepts, such as needs analysis, materials design, and course design through lecturing.

Vygotsky (1978) argued that people acquire knowledge through two kinds of activities: among people, and/or within ourselves. Considering the implications of these ideas for learning, individual and group-work activities were designed as a constructivist pedagogy that would promote intrapersonal and interpersonal dialogue about ESP-related concepts. After lecturing each ESP topic, the researcher set up tasks to be performed in pairs or small groups to promote socialisation. The participants kept journals for the researcher to check on their learning processes. They also read articles and books (e.g. Basturkmen, 2006, 2010; Hutchinson & Waters, 1987) and watched videos based on a list of topics covered.

The second component of the course involved moving from theory to practice. Following Vygotsky's (1978) theories, interpersonal dialogue that started in the classroom between student teachers and the course instructor was then expanded beyond the classroom. During Weeks 8-14, fieldwork was incorporated as the ideal constructivist practice into the regular ESP coursework to give learners direct experience beyond the classroom setting. Participants were assigned to perform a collaborative project in groups to gain a concrete real-life experience and to help them connect classroom learning to the world of ESP. Based on their own interests, each group designed an exemplary ESP course on their preferred ESP domain, developed a lesson plan, and performed micro-teaching in the lesson.

Whereas the former part of the ESP course provided the learners with a substantial amount of ESP knowledge, fieldwork was supported by ongoing and focussed guidance by the researcher to enhance effectiveness of pre-service teachers' socially constructed learning experiences. Fieldwork was a cooperative learning activity followed by a group presentation by the whole group with individual group members making a personal contribution. In this way, incorporated into the lecturing mode of instruction were various social learning activities, modelling, and direct experience, the basic concepts put forth by Vygotsky (1978) and Dewey (1929).

3. Results and discussion

In this section, findings from each research question are presented and discussed, supported by illustrative extracts from the questionnaires and student journals.

3.1. Turkish pre-service English language teachers' perceptions of ESP and ESP-related issues prior to the ESP teacher education course

Findings from the pre-test results and participants' journals revealed that prior to taking the course, most participants (96%) had no knowledge about ESP. This is illustrated by the following extract from Onur:

> "Actually, at first when I heard of ESP, I didn't know what it was. I wondered what we'd be doing during this course. I hoped that it'd be a different experience for me. I was extremely curious to experience the process myself".

Some participants hoped to experience something new and challenging, as reported by Mutlu:

> "I had no idea about what ESP is before, but I tried to guess what it could be because ESP stands for English for specific purposes. Then I thought maybe we'd teach professional knowledge in English. Engineering department was the first thing that came to my mind. I have friends there and they mention their English course is not the same as general English. Therefore, I predicted that this course would be different from others".

A minority of the participants (4%) appeared to have a general idea of ESP, as illustrated below by Arda:

"I knew that we'd study on specific purposes of learning/teaching English in different fields such as fine arts, medicine, engineering etc. From my point of view, it was going to teach me different aspects of English. Also, I was thinking that ESP course would help improve my teaching skills. Moreover, it'd raise our awareness towards English terms, phrases, etc.".

3.2. Turkish pre-service English language teachers' perception of ESP and ESP-related issues after participating in the ESP teacher education course

After completing the course, participants gained considerable knowledge on the fundamental components of ESP beyond their knowledge of English for general purposes, as illustrated below.

3.2.1. The meaning and origins of ESP

Seval expressed her opinion as:

"I've learned the origins of ESP. During 1960s, changes in the world resulted in the rising of ESP as a discipline. ESP is tailor-made because it focusses on the learners' specific needs. In addition, ESP developed in order to meet the needs of the New World".

Erdem provided a more detailed perspective:

"ESP does not focus on general English. It focusses on a particular field. For example tourism, business, medicine etc. ESP has a learning goal and the course is designed accordingly. It is learner centered. The main idea of ESP is to teach English in subjects that are needed for the students. This is really motivating for them because they can use what they have learned in the class in the real world. ESP students are generally adults".

3.2.2. Conducting needs analysis

The next most important area of knowledge gained concerned needs analysis. The participants had a clear understanding about the need to conduct needs analysis as a basis of ESP course design. Salih stated:

> "Thanks to the ESP course, I've learned the concept of needs analysis. I've learned that we should gather information about the learners' target situation and find their objective needs. We should gather personal information about the learners such as wants, and subjective needs. We should know the learners' lacks and gather professional information about how language and skills are used in the target situation".

It is evident from these reflections that participants learned not only the steps in conducting needs analysis but also the instruments used for collecting information about the ESP learners. One student teacher, Cem, reported: "We learned how to collect information using questionnaires, interviews, and observations". He added that needs analysis was his favourite topic and he felt confident about preparing and analysing a survey. When analysing survey results, he benefited from pie diagrams which he found enjoyable.

Another ESP group of students decided to conduct needs analysis for the mechanical engineering field. They reported that they created questions to identify ESP students' needs, their background, and English proficiency. They used Survey Monkey to apply the questionnaire on-line. They reached 17 students and analysed the results. Finally, they saw that students have difficulties especially in listening and speaking.

3.2.3. Materials design

Participants perceived developing ESP materials as a unique experience. Özge reported that it was the best part of the course for her as she liked creating something new. She specifically stated "I tried to put myself into these ESP students' positions while creating materials. I've gained knowledge and skill of making a unit on foods and drinks for the food engineering field". Participants also agreed that they became aware of the fact that ESP learners need tailor-made materials. Onur highlighted: "I have learned that not everyone learns English for the same aim and in the same way". In the tourism and hotel management vocational high school he explored that students learn different terms specific to their field. With this awareness, he prepared an original ESP material in collaboration with his group friends, designed activities, and planned a lesson.

Student teachers recognised the need to conduct needs analysis prior to developing materials. Özge reported:

> "Now, I know that I need to conduct needs analysis before starting to teach an ESP course. To state briefly, I learnt what I need to do to be able to run an ESP course in the future. It was an amazing experience in which we turned our theoretical knowledge into application".

Student teachers also expressed a feeling of confidence in producing ESP materials, as reported by Kaan:

> "I feel myself confident for conducting needs analysis, I can ask needed questions. I believe in myself that I can create an original ESP material for the intended courses thanks to my needs analysis. After learning what I need to do for them, I can teach them by doing my best".

3.3. The extent to which the Turkish pre-service English language teachers feel prepared to teach ESP in their future profession

While recognising the diversity of the ESP field, participants agreed that they gained sufficient knowledge and developed skills to enable them to teach ESP in the future. Onur mentioned:

> "Now that I understand the real meaning of ESP... Knowing ESP as a candidate teacher. For example I can design a lesson plan for any

Chapter 1

> profession to teach English. I can teach English to people and decide on materials suitable for them".

Student teachers became increasingly aware of the need to become more knowledgeable with regards to ESP, and building on their ESP knowledge and experience to deal with course requirements. One participant, Cem, believed that he could easily teach ESP in the future. He stated that he already had a degree in Computer Science, so teaching ESP in this field would be easy for him. He perceived other possibilities such as medical English as he previously studied physical therapy but dropped out of school for personal reasons. In general, students believed that thanks to knowledge and experience they gained in this course, they felt confident that they could easily adapt their teaching to different ESP teaching contexts.

Students admitted that in this project they mainly focussed on one ESP area, e.g. tourism or nursing. It would be unlikely that they would know all terms about any vocational area, but they would study hard to improve themselves. As Seval anticipated:

> "Teaching ESP requires knowing specific terms for example electrical circuit components (capacitor, diode etc.). I know electrical terms. That's why I won't have problems in this field. But in other fields of study (medicine, tourism) I may have problems".

Some students stated that they would have to refresh their knowledge in the future, building on their ESP teacher qualifications. Another participant, İpek, reported:

> "I can teach English in an ESP context. But I'll need to refresh my knowledge, terms, and vocabularies that are special to that field. Especially, I'll need to learn students' needs and lacks in learning English. I will also need to find different and helpful materials and activities that will make them active during the lessons. It can be much more challenging for me".

All students expressed a high level of satisfaction with the ESP course. Cem said: "We've learned lots of things about ESP which will be useful in my academic life. I've learned that there are many fields beyond general English. Now I'm aware of my full potential. Learning all these ideas makes me feel like a real ESP teacher". Another student, Salih, wanted to take advantage of it in the future. He reported: "Maybe, in future, I'll need to teach ESP and it won't be difficult for me thanks to this course".

In line with the constructivist paradigm, preparing the ESP project gave participants a concrete real-life experience, providing them with first-hand encounters within authentic contexts to apply concepts and principles to a new situation. Özge commented that the most useful experience for her and her group of friends was to observe a real ESP lesson in the faculty of law which helped her "to understand ESP better". Reflecting on her experience, she mentioned: "At the beginning of the process, I went to the Faculty of Law to observe the lesson of the ESP teacher". She, then, "interviewed the teacher and the students and took notes". While designing the ESP course, she considered students' levels, their lacks, and needs. Next, she made a list of the topics related to law and produced materials for two lessons and presented it as a micro-teaching lesson. Another interesting aspect of this project was to integrate technology in the material. She added: "I used Word Cloud composed of the key terms. I found micro-teaching challenging and the appropriate materials made the lesson fun. It was an exciting and unforgettable experience".

Belcher (2006) recognised that ESP teachers are specialists who are "often needs analysts first and foremost, then designers and implementers of specialised curricula" (p. 135). Similarly, student teachers in the present study recognised that an ESP teacher has many different roles, from course design to materials development. The following extract from Arda reflects the opinion of many students:

> "ESP teacher should always be a learner because needs are always changing. ESP teachers should develop themselves because they are a role model. They should be innovative, a researcher, and be connected with students so they can know what their students' needs are for learning

English. An ESP teacher should be a guide. Books are insufficient for teaching. So teachers should create new activities for students and encourage them towards the lesson. Knowing all these things makes ESP learning more effective".

In summary, student teachers appeared to have confidence in their abilities to conduct needs analysis, develop materials (adapting and/or producing materials), prepare a lesson plan, and micro-teach it. They appeared to have the capacity of applying such knowledge in predictable future ESP teaching situations. Student teachers also expressed an interest in exploring ways to extend their understanding of the subject area in the future. Generally, literature on needs analysis is concerned with determining objectives (Belcher, 2006). Similarly, all students recognised the importance of pre-course needs analysis, as well as the need to tailor instruction to learners' needs after a course has begun.

As it is evident from the section above, the present ESP course has provided an "understanding of abstract [ESP] concepts underlying practical [experience] in order to enable student teachers to adapt to novel situations and to apply their knowledge in [changing ESP] teaching contexts" (Hüttner, Smit, & Mehlmauer-Larcher, 2009, p. 100). Each ESP group, focussing on a different ESP topic, attempted to apply previously learned knowledge and experience to accomplish a particular goal or to solve a particular problem. At this point, and in line with Hyslop-Margison and Strobel (2007), pre-service teachers were engaged in a collaborative, real-life problem-based learning through project work, which is reinforced by the view that knowledge is essentially a socially constructed and negotiated product. During this fieldwork, pre-service teachers participated in expanded dialogue with ESP teachers and students to help them develop an informed but personal understanding of the subject. Findings from multiple sources suggest that through engaging in this type of dialogue, participants were able to construct a base of knowledge about the range of ESP topics, increase their awareness and competence on ESP-related topics, and that they developed an informed but personal understanding of the subject. As a consequence, they perceived themselves as well-prepared to teach ESP in their future profession.

4. Conclusions

Drawing on Vygotsky's (1978) concept of relational imitation and Dewey's (1929) notion of learning through direct experience, this study has presented a model for designing an ESP teacher education course for pre-service language teachers within the framework of constructivism. As noted by Hüttner et al. (2009), while so many English language teachers are working in the field of ESP, many new teachers are coming into the field too. These newcomers need to be given some ESP-related education in the teacher education programmes. It is therefore essential that ESP be taught in pre-service teacher education to prepare prospective teacher candidates for the world of ESP teaching professions. Findings gained from the implementation of this ESP course at a Turkish university suggest that the approach followed in this study could fruitfully be adapted to other teacher education programmes.

Acknowledgements

I would like to thank all the participants who took part in this study. I would also like to acknowledge the Scientific Research and Development Unit of Çukurova University, Adana, Turkey, that funded this research with Project Number SBA-2017 9446.

References

Basturkmen, H. (2006). *Ideas and options in English for specific purposes*. Lawrence Erlbaum Associates.
Basturkmen, H. (2010). *Developing courses in English for specific purposes*. Palgrave Macmillan.
Basturkmen, H. (2014). LSP teacher education: review of literature and suggestions for the research agenda. *Iberica, 28*, 17-34.
Basturkmen, H. (2017). ESP teacher education needs. *Language Teaching,* (First View), 1-13.

Belcher, D. (2006). English for specific purposes: teaching to the perceived needs and imagined futures in worlds of work, study and everyday life. *TESOL Quarterly, 40*(1), 133-156. https://doi.org/10.2307/40264514

Creswell, J. W. (2013). *Qualitative inquiry and research design: choosing among five traditions* (3rd ed.). Sage.

Dewey, J. (1929). *The sources of a science of education.* Horace Liveright.

Hughes, A. S., & Sears, A. (2004). Situated learning and anchored instruction as vehicles for social education. In A. Sears & I. Wright (Eds), *Challenges and prospects for Canadian social studies* (pp. 259-273). Pacific Educational Press.

Hutchinson, T., & Waters, A. (1987). *English for specific purposes.* Cambridge University Press.

Hüttner, J., Smit, U., & Mehlmauer-Larcher, B. (2009). ESP teacher education at the interface of theory and practice: introducing a model of mediated corpus-based genre analysis. *System, 37*(1), 99-109. https://doi.org/10.1016/j.system.2008.06.003

Hyslop-Margison, E. J., & Sears, A. (2006). *Neo-liberalism, globalization and human capital learning: reclaiming education for democratic citizenship.* Springer.

Hyslop-Margison, E. J., & Strobel, J. (2007). Constructivism and education: misunderstandings and pedagogical implications. *The Teacher Educator, 43*(1), 72-86. https://doi.org/10.1080/08878730701728945

Smith, J. (2001). Modelling the social construction of knowledge in ELT teacher education. *ELT Journal, 55*(3), 221-227. https://doi.org/10.1093/elt/55.3.221

Vygotsky, L. (1978). *Mind in society: the development of higher psychological processes.* Harvard University Press.

2 Finding the way through the ESP maze: designing an ESP teacher education programme

Elis Kakoulli Constantinou[1], Salomi Papadima-Sophocleous[2], and Nicos Souleles[3]

Abstract

English for Specific Purposes (ESP) is an area of language education that has been advancing during the last years due to increased social and professional mobility. Despite this, as shown in the related literature, the area of ESP Teacher Education (TE) is deprived of attention by researchers; as a result, many ESP educators in different countries are General English (GE) teachers with insufficient training in ESP. The present chapter reports on the first findings of a technical action research study, which aims at exploring and addressing the problem of insufficient ESP TE among a specific group of ESP practitioners, suggesting an intervention in the form of an online ESP TE programme. Following the spiral pattern of action research, the study evolves in cycles of continuous improvement. This chapter focusses on the initial stages of the study during which the problem of lack of ESP TE opportunities was identified, and a remedy to this problem, an online ESP TE course, named Online Reflective Teacher Education in ESP (ReTEESP Online), was developed and piloted before its implementation.

Keywords: English for specific purposes, teacher education, technical action research, reflection, online instruction.

1. Cyprus University of Technology, Limassol, Cyprus; elis.constantinou@cut.ac.cy; https://orcid.org/0000-0001-8854-3816

2. Cyprus University of Technology, Limassol, Cyprus; salomi.papadima@cut.ac.cy; https://orcid.org/0000-0003-4444-4482

3. Cyprus University of Technology, Limassol, Cyprus; nicos.souleles@cut.ac.cy; https://orcid.org/0000-0002-1059-942X

How to cite this chapter: Kakoulli Constantinou, E., Papadima-Sophocleous, S., & Souleles, N. (2019). Finding the way through the ESP maze: designing an ESP teacher education programme. In S. Papadima-Sophocleous, E. Kakoulli Constantinou & C. N. Giannikas (Eds), *ESP teaching and teacher education: current theories and practices* (pp. 27-46). Research-publishing.net. https://doi.org/10.14705/rpnet.2019.33.924

Chapter 2

1. Introduction

Almost 60 years after the emergence of ESP (Dudley-Evans & St John, 1998), the economic, political, social, and technological changes that have occurred around the globe have led to an increase in the numbers of people who attend ESP courses. ESP, with all its subdivisions, e.g. English for Occupational Purposes, English for Academic Purposes (EAP), etc., is a field which is currently thriving. Nevertheless, a review of the literature in the field of ESP TE illustrates a lack of research in the area of ESP TE and the need for more ESP TE opportunities which meet the needs of ESP practitioners. This problem in the area of ESP TE exists across the ESP practitioners' communities in many parts of the world (Abedeen, 2015; Bracaj, 2014; Chostelidou, Griva, & Tsakiridou, 2009; Sifakis, 2005), and it is also sensed in the researchers' own context.

Despite the fact that differences between ESP and GE teaching methodology are not significant (Dudley-Evans & St John, 1998), the specialised nature of ESP and its focus on learners' needs give distinctive attributes to the role of ESP educators. As a consequence, the provision of ESP TE is essential, a fact that has been widely acknowledged in the literature (Abedeen, 2015; Basturkmen, 2010; Bell, 2002; Bezukladnikov & Kruze, 2012; Bojović, 2006; Bracaj, 2014; Chen, 2012; Howard, 1997; Johnstone, 1997; Mahapatra, 2011). Nevertheless, despite the differences between them, language teachers mostly receive training focussed on general English Language Teaching (ELT) and not ESP.

Some research studies conducted in the area of ESP TE describe what ESP TE opportunities should involve, how they should be delivered (Abedeen, 2015; Bojović, 2006; Jackson, 1998; Johnstone, 1997; Master, 1997; Mebitil, 2011; Savas, 2009), and outline the kind of knowledge, competences, and skills ESP practitioners should acquire to be successful. Furthermore, they provide advice on the different conventions practitioners need to be familiar with, and elaborate on the ways in which this can be achieved. Drawing on this research, the present study aimed at providing a solution to the problem of insufficient ESP TE that a group of ESP practitioners faced. The solution proposed was an intervention in the form of an online ESP TE programme. The present chapter aims at presenting the pilot implementation of the programme. The purpose of the study was to investigate the effectiveness of the programme, the challenges participants faced, and the improvements that needed to be made.

2. ReTEESP Online and the context of the research study

A review of the literature as well as an analysis of ESP practitioners' needs in terms of ESP TE (Kakoulli Constantinou & Papadima-Sophocleous, under review) showed that the most appropriate solution to address the needs of the particular group of ESP practitioners was the design of an educational intervention, a short-term online ESP TE course founded on a 'practise what you preach' approach inspired by Wallace's (1991) reflective model of TE, based on principles of ESP and the theories of social constructivism and connectivism. Apart from providing information on the content of the course, the literature review and the needs analysis process indicated that the ESP TE course should be delivered online due to practical issues related to flexibility and cost effectiveness (Jung, 2005). The option of attending an online ESP TE course that did not demand the participants' physical presence was more attractive, and furthermore, it provided the opportunity to ESP practitioners from different educational contexts to participate and share experiences. The course created was an online reflective TE course in ESP, named ReTEESP Online.

The current influence of cloud computing in education, and the cost effectiveness, practicality, flexibility, and high scalability of such tools (Kakoulli Constantinou, 2018), were the main reasons Google's cloud computing services for educational purposes, the G Suite for Education, were selected as the most appropriate means to deliver ReTEESP Online (also see Barlow & Lane, 2007; Herrick, 2009; Railean, 2012). The suite had been previously integrated in two EAP courses for first-year students of the Departments of Agricultural Sciences, Biotechnology, and Food Science and Commerce, Finance, and Shipping at the Cyprus University of Technology during the academic years 2016-2017 and 2017-2018 (Kakoulli Constantinou, 2018, 2019), and even though the context in

Chapter 2

those cases was different, the researchers gained valuable insights regarding the qualities and affordances of the suite.

ReTEESP Online was designed to be a three-week (maximum six), five-hour per week, free course, intended for (1) ESP educators representing different ESP fields, (2) EFL educators who would like to educate themselves on issues pertaining to ESP teaching methodology, or (3) practitioners looking to update their knowledge on the latest developments in ESP teaching practices. The aim of the course was to engage educators in hands-on activities involving both synchronous and asynchronous communication that would enable them to develop in areas associated with ESP teaching and give them the opportunity to implement their new knowledge in their ESP practice. The course was flexible, depending on the participants' profiles and needs, and it evolved around topics such as ESP and its characteristics, the ESP lesson planning process, ESP students' needs analysis, resources, tools, and tasks for the ESP classroom, the ESP lesson in practice and collaborative reflection on the teaching process. It was based on a reflective model for professional development and a 'practise what you preach' approach (Wallace, 1991), since the techniques and methods of instruction which were used in the course could be used by trainees in their language classrooms. The course adopted a social constructivist perspective to teacher training, taking into account the social context in which the ESP practitioners operate, being based on discussion and a constant exchange of ideas and collaboration (Roberts, 1998). Finally, it was also governed by principles of connectivism, which supports that knowledge is acquired through making connections and extending one's personal network (Downes, 2010; Siemens, 2005).

3. Method

3.1. Methodology

The study employed technical action research, which is the type of action research that aims at improving the educational practice by making it more efficient and effective, and the practitioners depend on the researcher, who acts as a facilitator, in order to improve the educational practice (Denscombe, 1998; Grundy, 1982). As aforementioned, this chapter describes the findings of the pilot implementation of the study, following Vaccarino, Comrie, Murray, and Sligo's (2007, pp. 14-27) description of the pilot stage of an action research study in the context of The Wanganui Adult Literacy and Employment project. For validation purposes, a 'critical friend' (McNiff, 2002) was engaged consistently with looking at the research from time to time and providing the researchers with critical feedback.

3.2. Data collection tools

Data was elicited through an online questionnaire administered to the participants at the beginning of the course as well as ESP practitioners' reflective journals and comments throughout the course. Moreover, data was also collected through the course facilitator's field notes and focus group discussions which took place after the course completion. The data gathered was mainly qualitative and was analysed using NVivo software for qualitative data analysis.

The coding process was repeated by the external researcher who acted as a 'critical friend' (McNiff, 2002), in order to enhance credibility and validity, avoid research bias, and rule out any misinterpretation of the data. Cohen's (1960) kappa test was run to determine inter-rater reliability, in other words if there was agreement between the researchers' and the second rater's thematic analysis of the data. The results showed that there was almost perfect agreement between the two coders' judgements, $k=.866$, $p<.0005$ (Landis & Koch, 1977).

3.3. Participants

The pilot implementation of ReTEESP Online ran from May 2nd to June 29th, 2017, with six ESP practitioners from Higher Education (HE), who represented a convenience sample, a sample which the researcher had easy access to (inspired by Cohen, Manion, & Morrison, 2000). Despite the low number of participants, the large amount of data gathered and the triangulation techniques used in the study (use of four different research tools) allowed the extraction of in depth results. To ensure the anonymity of the participants, they were referred to as Teachers 1-6. Table 1 presents some information related to the participants.

Table 1. The participants

Participants: HE ESP instructors	Country of origin	Age
Teacher 1	Spain	30-39
Teacher 2	Cyprus	30-39
Teacher 3	Cyprus	40-49
Teacher 4	Greece	30-39
Teacher 5	Cyprus	40-49
Teacher 6	Cyprus	40-49

All participants had previous experience in teaching ESP ranging from one to 20 years and appeared to be very active in the ESP field, both in terms of teaching ESP and in terms of conducting research in the field. Four participants had an extensive background of teaching experiences. Two of the practitioners were also pursuing a PhD in the ESP field at the time.

4. Results and discussion

The findings from this trial implementation of ReTEESP Online generated important implications for the future refinement and improvement of the course.

The analysis of the data, which was coded and categorised, yielded three general thematic categories. These categories were: (1) participants' profiles, (2) the course experience, and (3) suggestions for improvement of the course. Each of these general categories consisted of a series of subcategories, which consisted of other subcategories, as they appear in Table 2.

Table 2. The thematic categories which resulted from the analysis of data

A. Participants' profiles	B. The course experience	C. Suggestions for improvement of the course
1. Who they are	1. The course content	1. Content
2. Reasons for attending the course	• Course material	• Organisation
	• Tasks	• Tasks
3. Challenges they face with teaching ESP	• Topics	2. Presentation of material
4. Beliefs about ESP learners	2. Positive aspects of the course	• Facilitator's presence
	• Elements liked	3. Duration of the course
	• Knowledge acquired	• Deadlines
	• Practices from the course that can be integrated in ESP	4. Technology tools
		• Facebook closed group
	• Participants' realisations	• Participants' technology literacy
	• Participants' high performance in the course	5. Collaborative work
	3. Challenges faced during the course	• Pairing/organisation into groups
	• Participants' expectations from the course	6. Reflections
		7. Communication with participants
	• Collaboration	
	• Participants' failure to meet the deadlines	8. Participants' motivations
	• Negative feelings created	
	• Cases in which knowledge was not acquired	
	• Difficulties faced during the use of certain tools	
	• Changes in plans	

4.1. Participants' profiles

The first thematic category, which relates to the six participants' profiles (as presented in Table 2), revealed the following in relation to the four themes that emerged from the data:

> (1) Only one of the participants had received training in ESP as part of their Bachelor of Arts (BA), while the other five had received training on ESP as part of in-service and in the context of conferences and seminars, and that was another reason that made the course attractive.

> (2) All participants were very actively involved in conference participation and seminar attendance, and they all tried to keep abreast of the latest developments in the field. They wished to expand their knowledge about ESP teaching and developing teaching materials and also to exchange and share ideas with other colleagues, reflect on them and also to discuss different challenges faced in their everyday teaching in a collective effort to provide solutions. All of them sought to update themselves on the latest developments in the ESP field, and they had a positive attitude towards the idea of continuous professional development.

> (3) Teacher 2 identified finding and designing appropriate material which will serve the purpose of the courses that she taught as the major challenge that she faced in her ESP teaching. Despite the fact that relevant material can be found on the internet, according to her "it is never spot on what [she is] looking for". Adapting the material is difficult since, as she added, ESP practitioners are not experts in the area. The same challenge was acknowledged by Teachers 3 and 5. Teacher 3 also added that adapting the material to meet the level of her students meant that the material was not authentic any more. Moreover, Teachers 1, 5, and 6 also stressed the importance of having substantial discipline-related knowledge, which made designing and implementing courses more demanding and sometimes overwhelming for teachers.

(4) In the focus group discussion after the completion of the course, Teacher 1 expressed the belief that students like to remain in their comfort zone and that her job was to take them out of there by engaging them in tasks that would lead them outside the four walls of the classroom, in real-life situations. Furthermore, Teachers 2, 3, and 5 expressed the view that, with no appropriate control by the instructor, students are not engaged in collaborative tasks, but they prefer working individually instead.

4.2. The course experience

The second thematic category that emerged from the data concentrated on a description of the ESP participants' and the facilitator's experiences from the implementation of the course. As far as the positive aspects of the course are concerned, during the focus group discussions, participants generally expressed the view that the course was well-structured and well-organised and it guided them step-by-step through all the tasks. Moreover, they stated that the facilitator's idea of organising them into pairs worked very well. Collaboration among the participants was reported as enjoyable, despite the fact that some said that future participants in the course might express some concerns on the issues of collaboration and sharing, mostly having to do with sharing one's own work. Regarding the ESP lesson plan, which participants were asked to produce and implement in their classes in the context of the course, the fact that the course facilitator had separated the process into different steps gave time to the participants to work on the process and reflect on it thoroughly.

The findings from the facilitator's field notes, the participants' reflective journals, and the focus group discussions revealed that all six participants in the course liked the instructional technology tools that were used, that is Google Classroom, Google Drive, MindMeister, the closed Facebook group, and Skype. These were considered as effective, in the sense that they served the purposes which the course facilitator used them for. Simultaneously, the facilitator thought that these tools were flexible, easy to use, and well-accepted by the participants. In one of the focus group discussions after the completion of the course, Teacher 1 says:

> "I really liked, like the interface and how you can go to the stream and see what's happening, see whether you have submitted your work or not, and the layout is very, it's very nice. I hadn't used it before (laughs)... and it was great. We use Google and Google's best tools for a project but not yet Google Classroom and it's very nice. And then everything was very clear from the very beginning, very well-organised, well you know, I didn't get lost in the... you know how sometimes online courses can be very... overwhelming because you don't know where things are, or you don't know how to navigate the web pages. Well it wasn't the case with this course. So, from the very beginning and the introduction everything was very clear and well-organised".

Teacher 4 agrees, adding the following:

> "Yeah, I agree and I think that it was really a good idea to use Facebook as a different kind of platform, a bit more informal, a bit more communicative, not that it wasn't interactive in the classroom (Google Classroom) but we also had something else um to... er I mean you used it for announcements sort of let us know when something new was up in the course so I thought it was a good outlet and I've used Facebook with my ESP courses before, and it was very well-received by the students, and they enjoyed using it and they became very interactive with each other, and they used it to be informed about the course as you did with us, and I thought that was a good way, um to communicate with everyone instead of the standard you know email and this happening and that happening...".

All six participants also positively welcomed the opportunity to remember how a well-structured lesson plan is designed and the fact that the course combined both a theoretical part (the list of useful readings that the participants were provided with) and a practical part, which involved the implementation of the lesson plan participants had designed. They learned about new learning theories such as connectivism, which they had not heard of in the past, but also remembered some important principles of ESP. They also liked the progress report that the facilitator compiled somewhere in the middle of the course, in order, on the one hand, to inform participants about their progress, and, on the other hand, to urge those who were behind to complete their unfinished work.

Two of the participants in the course admitted that they gained a lot from the interaction and the exchange of ideas, and that they integrated new things in their courses that they were not aware of previously. Almost all of the participants expressed the view that they benefited from the reflective processes of the course, since reflection made them think about their careers as ESP practitioners, their teaching contexts, their teaching practices, the different roles they assume as ESP practitioners, and the training they had received in developing and delivering ESP courses to a wide range of HE students from different disciplines. Moreover, the course provided them with material and specific tasks they could apply in their ESP classes (e.g. useful readings on which they could base their teaching, sample lesson plans, links where they could find material, etc.) in the new academic year, and also a new understanding in several things. At the same time, the course facilitator's field notes revealed that the constant interaction and exchange of ideas, and also the whole process of checking the participants' work and providing feedback to them, were very enlightening for the facilitator too; after the completion of the course, she too felt that she had gained new knowledge and ideas she could implement in her own ESP teaching classes.

Teacher 4 states the following in one of the focus groups discussions after the completion of the course:

> "Well, for me I feel I benefited from the course because I learned new things I can apply in my teaching coming September (she laughs). It's like, I got information I can immediately use and it wasn't random, it wasn't general, it was very specific things that I could apply in my teaching when I'm teaching any department really, so that was the biggest benefit for me... that I had actual material that I can put forward and I also have a new understanding in several things that I hadn't thought of before... and I can plan it, I can plan my lesson accordingly now and also integrate new things that I hadn't been using before".

On the other hand, the participants also faced challenges. Some of them expressed the view that their expectations were not completely met; these were ESP practitioners that had a similar background as the course facilitator and researcher, therefore one could assume that they were already familiar with the things included in the course, and they expected to be exposed to new ideas. On the contrary, the two ESP practitioners who came from different backgrounds and different teaching contexts did not appear to have any other expectations from the course.

Another challenge that participants faced was related to working together to complete the collaborative tasks and failure to meet deadlines. This is reflected in both the facilitator's reflective journal and the focus group discussions, and it resulted in the extension of the course. They all agreed on the fact that the reason behind this was their workload as well as their other commitments in combination with lack of free time. This might imply that the course was overloaded with materials and tasks, and that participants could not cope with them. In one of the focus groups discussions, Teacher 2 states:

> "It was a matter of workload. Maybe if I didn't have so much workload, if I didn't have so much pressure, maybe I could focus more on the things you assigned to us".

Teachers 3, 4, and 5 also admitted that they did not study carefully some of the material the facilitator had uploaded for them on the platform, again due to lack of time. When files and documents were uploaded on the platform they just scanned through them, missing points that the facilitator considered to be important for the educational process, and paying attention to presentations or materials which were more concise instead of reading useful articles and large word documents. This fact yielded important implications concerning changes that had to be made too.

Another reason which explains this constant extension of deadlines might also be culture. Teacher 1 admitted that the same thing also happened with her students, and she characterised it as a "Mediterranean thing". As the course proceeded, the course facilitator's field notes reveal that a few of them started feeling overwhelmed by the course because of the workload. This is also displayed in the focus group discussions, where two of them (Teachers 2 and 5) admitted that they felt extremely stressed when they had to describe their teaching practices on the basis of theories of learning. They found this a difficult task to do, and 'complained' that the level of performance of a couple of participants in the course was too high, and this created feelings of stress and fear of inferiority.

Finally, some practical difficulties regarding the use of certain technology tools were mentioned in the facilitator's field notes, the participants' reflective journals, and the focus group discussions. A challenge that was noted mostly by the facilitator was the fact that due to the practical difficulties faced by the participants during the course (e.g. the sound on a PowerPoint presentation was not working, participants forgetting passwords, connection problems during Skype Webinars, etc.), she had to be flexible, constantly alert, and make different changes in the course while it was taking place. This was not something unexpected, since changes of instructional plans is a practice that occurs in all sorts of teaching contexts.

4.3. Suggestions for improvement of the course

The third major thematic category that derived from the data related to suggestions for the improvement of the course. As Table 2 illustrates, the suggestions expressed by the participants and the facilitator revolved around five major themes: (1) the content of the course, (2) the presentation of material, (3) the duration of the course, (4) the technology tools used for the delivery of the course, (5) collaborative work, (6) reflective procedures, (7) communication with participants, and (8) participants' motivations.

As far as the content of the course is concerned, data from the participants' reflective journals and focus groups indicated that the course was found overwhelming and hectic in terms of content by four of the participants. Moreover, Teacher 3 suggested that it would have been a lot better if the facilitator provided the participants with different practical ideas on where to find material for their classes and how to conduct needs analysis, and perhaps even provide them with ready-made questionnaires. In addition, as noted in the facilitator's field notes, the facilitator also suggested that it would have been useful for the participants to be introduced to different ESP organisations/networks/social media groups that they could be members of as well as conferences on ESP in order to expand their network and develop further. Moreover, according to the course facilitator, ideas on resources and materials could have been added earlier in the course, before participants had started working on their ESP lesson plans so that they would have an idea on where and how to look for their scenarios, tasks, etc.

As far as the presentation of the material is concerned, in one of the focus group discussions, Teachers 3 and 5 supported that material should be easily accessible and comprehensive but concise. Furthermore, they suggested that the facilitator should present the material in video tutorials, as this would give the course a more personal nature and would make it more interesting.

Regarding the duration of the course, in the focus group discussions, both the participants (all six of them) and the facilitator shared the view that increasing the duration in order to allow more time for the participants to complete the tasks would not be wise, because there might be participants who will not be willing to continue the course for too long. They suggested having participants engage in shorter and more concise tasks that can be completed in a short period of time, combining some of the units so that the course shrinks, and sending kind reminders to the participants that have missed deadlines. Another idea suggested by Teacher 2 was having a set day for submissions. Finally, Teacher 6 expressed the view that having a minimum and a maximum time of duration and allowing for flexibility within that period of time could be another solution to the problem. It should always depend on the audience, their commitments, and needs.

Regarding the technology tools used for the delivery of the course, the suggestions expressed by the participants were the following: first of all, in the focus group discussions, to eliminate the problem of having two Google accounts (one personal and one for the course), Teacher 2 suggested synchronising the Google accounts provided by the facilitator with the participants' personal Google accounts. That would make it easier for them to see all the notifications posted by the facilitator. Secondly, Teacher 6 expressed the opinion that the Google Drive folder should have been more structured, with all the folders needed created by the facilitator from the beginning of the course. A tutorial or a video clip might be needed to guide participants on how to use the tools that will be needed for the course. Furthermore, participants' presence in the closed Facebook group after the completion of the course was regarded as a good idea, since the network built would continue to exist this way.

In relation to collaboration, Teachers 3, 5, and 6 suggested that some of the tasks could be delivered individually instead of collaboratively, and that sharing should not be applied to all the stages of the course. This stemmed from the participants' concerns regarding sharing their personal work and ideas, and also from the practical difficulties they faced during collaboration. Moreover, to eliminate the possibility of participants working on tasks separately, Teacher 3 suggested that the facilitator could assign pieces of the work that can be finished only when other participants step in.

On the issue of reflection, it was suggested that a folder for their reflections should be created from the beginning of the course so that the participants are not lost in the cloud; this was suggested by Teacher 6 in the focus group discussions. Moreover, in the same focus group, another participant (Teacher 3) stated that the questions posed to enact reflection were repetitive, and they needed to be more specific every time. Finally, Teacher 6 suggested that constant reflection following every single unit might be unnecessary and might cause repetition.

As far as issues related to communication with participants are concerned, the facilitator's field notes revealed details that could minimize certain practical constraints, e.g. participants being notified before the course commences about the tools that will be used for communication so that they create Skype accounts on time, in case they do not have them. Furthermore, Google Calendar should be used for the deadlines of tasks, and it should be made known to the participants at the beginning of the course.

Last but not least, regarding motivation enhancement, all participants in the course suggested having some kind of reward for the end of the course, something the participants can look forward to, such as a membership in an ESP organisation, a book, or a voucher, which could motivate the participants and reduce potential withdrawals from the course. Selection of the winner could be done by draw, and all participants should be provided with certificates of attendance.

5. Conclusions

This chapter has presented the initial stage of a technical action research study which emerged from the need of ESP instructors for ESP TE. This first trial implementation of the intervention proposed yielded important results for its refinement and improvement for the next stage of this study, and despite the constraints of technical action research, it might provide useful insights to future endeavours in the field of ESP TE.

Notwithstanding the limitations of any type of action research, in this case technical action research, which rest with its inherent nature to provide solutions that can be applied in a particular context, in comparison to other research methods that aim at generalising results, the benefits of action research are many. Coming from a more modernised and more socially oriented stream of thought, the value of any action research study rests on the fact that, through the whole process, both the participants and the researchers grow professionally, gaining enlightenment and deeper understanding of themselves and the social or professional environment they operate in through practice and reflection. Such examples of research constitute 'bodies of case study evidence', and according to McNiff (2002), "the more case studies that appear, the more powerful the body of knowledge becomes" (p. 26).

In this sense, the value of this technical action research study lies in the fact that the researchers together with the participants in the study underwent a transformational journey which involved the development of ideas and insights by all the participants in relation to ESP teaching practices. Furthermore, the present study generated findings that related to the profiles of ESP practitioners in tertiary education and their needs in terms of ESP TE, the content, technology tools, and generally the nature that an online reflective ESP TE could have, parametres that could be positively perceived by ESP practitioners in ESP TE contexts, and others that could constitute challenges. Finally, the study presented useful suggestions for future ESP TE endeavours considering the specific needs of ESP practitioners as well as their teaching contexts. These results may yield some potential implications for future attempts in the field of ESP TE.

Acknowledgements

We would like to thank all the colleagues who participated in this research study. Special thanks to Dr Antigoni Parmaxi for her constructive feedback throughout the study.

References

Abedeen, F. (2015). *Exploration of ESP teacher knowledge and practices at tertiary and applied colleges in Kuwait: implications for pre- and in-service ESP teacher training.* Exeter. https://ore.exeter.ac.uk/repository/bitstream/handle/10871/17437/AbedeenF.pdf?sequence=1

Barlow, K., & Lane, J. (2007). Like technology from an advanced alien culture: Google Apps for Education at ASU. *35th Annual ACM SIGUCCS Fall Conference*, 8–10. https://doi.org/10.1145/1294046.1294049

Basturkmen, H. (2010). *Developing courses in English for specific purposes.* Palgrave Macmillan.

Bell, D. (2002). Help! I've been asked to teach a class on ESP. *IATEFL Voices, 169 Oct/Nov.* http://www.esp-world.info/!encyclopaedia/IATEFL%20Issues%20169%20-%20Help!%20I%27ve%20been%20asked%20to%20teach%20a%20class%20on%20ESP.htm

Bezukladnikov, K., & Kruze, B. (2012). An outline of an ESP teacher training course. *World Applied Sciences Journal, 20* (Special Issue of Pedagogy and Psychology), 103-106.

Bojović, M. (2006). Teaching foreign language for specific purposes: teacher development. In M. Brejc (Ed.), *Co-operative partnerships in teacher education proceedings of the 31st annual ATEE conference, Slovenia* (pp. 1-3). National School for Leadership in Education. http://www.pef.uni-lj.si/atee/

Bracaj, M. (2014). Teaching English for specific purposes and teacher training. *European Scientific Journal, 10*(2), 40-49.

Chen, Y. (2012). ESP development in Taiwan: an overview. *ESP News*, TESOL International Association (August). http://newsmanager.commpartners.com/tesolespis/issues/2012-08-21/2.html

Chostelidou, D., Griva, E., & Tsakiridou, E. (2009). A Record of the training needs of ESP practitioners in vocational education. In *Selected Papers from the 18th ISTAL* (pp. 131-143). http://www.enl.auth.gr/symposium18/papers/14_CHOSTELIDOU_GRIVA_TSAKIRIDOU.pdf

Cohen, J. (1960). A coefficient of agreement for nominal scales. *Educational and Psychological Measurement, 20*, 37-46.

Cohen, L., Manion, L., & Morrison, K. (2000). *Research methods in education*. Routledge.

Denscombe, M. (1998). *The good research guide* (4th ed.). McGraw-Hill and Open University Press.

Downes, S. (2010). New technology supporting informal learning. *Journal of Emerging Technologies in Web Intelligence, 2*(1), 27-33. https://doi.org/10.4304/jetwi.2.1.27-33

Dudley-Evans, T., & St John, M. J. (1998). *Developments in English for specific purposes: a multi-disciplinary approach*. Cambridge University Press.

Grundy, S. (1982). Three modes of action research. *Curriculum Perspectives, 2*(3), 23-34.

Herrick, D. R. (2009). Google this! Using Google apps for collaboration and productivity. *Proceedings of the 37th Annual ACM SIGUCCS Fall Conference*, 55–64. https://doi.org/10.1145/1629501.1629513

Howard, R. (1997). LSP in the UK. In R. Howard & G. Brown (Eds), *Teacher education for LSP* (pp. 55-57). Multilingual Matters.

Jackson, J. (1998). Reality-based decision cases in ESP teacher education: windows on practice. *English for Specific Purposes, 17*(2), 151-167. http://doi.org/10.1016/S0889-4906(97)00004-5

Johnstone, R. (1997). LSP teacher education (foreign languages): common and specific elements. In R. Howard & G. Brown (Eds), *Teacher education for LSP* (pp. 11-21). Multilingual Matters.

Jung, I. (2005). Cost-effectiveness of online teacher training. *Open Learning, 20*(2), 131-146.

Kakoulli Constantinou, E. (2018). Teaching in clouds: using the G Suite for Education for the delivery of two EAP courses. *The Journal of Teaching English for Specific and Academic Purposes, 6*(2), Special Issue, 305-317. https://doi.org/10.22190/jtesap1802305c

Kakoulli Constantinou, E. (2019). Revisiting the cloud: reintegrating the G Suite for Education in ESP teaching. In C. N. Giannikas, E. Kakoulli Constantinou & S. Papadima Sophocleous (Eds.), *Professional development in CALL: a selection of papers* (pp. 55-69). Research-publishing.net. https://doi.org/10.14705/rpnet.2019.28.870

Kakoulli Constantinou, E., & Papadima-Sophocleous, S. (under review). ESP teacher education: examining the profiles of English for specific purposes practitioners and analysing their needs.

Landis, J. R., & Koch, G. G. (1977). The measurement of observer agreement for categorical data. *Biometrics, 33*, 159-174.

Mahapatra, S. K. (2011). Teacher training in ESP: a historical review. *English for Specific Purposes World, 11*(33), 1-15.

Master, P. (1997). ESP teacher education in the USA. In R. Howard & G. Brown (Eds), *Teacher education for LSP* (pp. 22-40). Multilingual Matters.

McNiff, J. (2002). *Action research for professional development. Concise advice for new action researchers* (3rd ed.). http://www.jeanmcniff.com/ar-booklet.asp

Mebitil, N. (2011). *An exploration of the main difficulties, challenges and requirements of the ESP teaching situation in Algeria: The case of ESP teachers at Abou Bekr Belkaid University, Tlemcen*. Abou Bekr Belkaid University – Tlemcen. http://dspace.univ-tlemcen.dz/bitstream/112/317/1/AN-EXPLORATION-OF-THE-MAIN-DIFFICULTIES-CHALLENGES-AND-REQUIREMENTS-OF-THE-ESP-TEACHING-SITUATION-IN-ALGERIA.THE-CASE-OF-ESP-TEACHERS-AT-ABOUBEKR-BELKAID.pdf

Railean, E. (2012). Google Apps for Education – a powerful solution for global scientific classrooms with learner centred environment. *International Journal of Computer Science Research and Application, 2*(2), 19-27.

Roberts, J. (1998). *Language teacher education*. Arnold.

Savas, B. (2009). Role of functional academic literacy in ESP teaching: ESP teacher training in Turkey for sustainable development. *The Journal of International Social Research, 2*(9), 395-406.

Siemens, G. (2005). Connectivism: a learning theory for the digital age. *International Journal of Instructional Technology and Distance Learning, 2*(1), 3-10.

Sifakis, N. C. (2005). English for specific and academic purposes - a trendy demand? Orientations in ESP/EAP research, with a critical perspective on the Greek situation. In F. Perdiki, E. Panourgia, E. Vergidou & K. Samara (Eds), *Teaching foreign languages for specific purposes: a trend ora demand? 1st ESP Conference in Kavala - Conference Proceedings* (pp. 17-30). TEI of Kavala.

Vaccarino, F., Comrie, M., Murray, N., & Sligo, F. (2007). *Action research reflections: the Wanganui adult literacy and employment project.* Massey University.

Wallace, M. J. (1991). *Training foreign language teachers. A reflective approach.* Cambridge University Press.

3 Self-scaffolding and the role of new technologies in ESP teacher education

Irena Aleksić-Hajduković[1], Danka Sinadinović[2], and Stevan Mijomanović[3]

Abstract

This research aims to explore how English for Specific Purposes (ESP) teachers and practitioners utilise new technologies, e.g. Massive Open Online Courses (MOOCs), webinars, online platforms, etc. as a means of self-scaffolding in order to exceed their threshold in pedagogical, linguistic, and discoursal competencies in various ESP domains. The current study analyses the data provided by ESP teachers and practitioners from various educational backgrounds. The findings obtained via a questionnaire show to what extent ESP teachers and practitioners exploit new technologies as a means of self-scaffolding, but also offer a classification of the tools, strategies, and opportunities available for their self-directed professional development. Furthermore, various electronic self-scaffolding resources are discussed and evaluated according to their accessibility, applicability, and popularity among teachers. While this research is not concerned with cross-cultural differences in ESP teacher education, broadly speaking, it is concerned with gathering data from various teaching environments with a view to providing a universal representation of current trends in ESP teacher education. Offering an up-to-date model for ESP teacher education is an important implication of this research whose findings could serve as guidelines and contribute to material development.

---

1. University of Belgrade, Belgrade, Serbia; irena.aleksic@stomf.bg.ac.rs; https://orcid.org/0000-0002-1884-4784

2. University of Belgrade, Belgrade, Serbia; dankas78@gmail.com; https://orcid.org/0000-0002-3643-5917

3. University of Belgrade, Belgrade, Serbia; stevan.mijomanovic@gmail.com; https://orcid.org/0000-0002-2472-0016

How to cite this chapter: Aleksić-Hajduković, I., Sinadinović, D., & Mijomanović, S. (2019). Self-scaffolding and the role of new technologies in ESP teacher education. In S. Papadima-Sophocleous, E. Kakoulli Constantinou & C. N. Giannikas (Eds), *ESP teaching and teacher education: current theories and practices* (pp. 47-62). Research-publishing.net. https://doi.org/10.14705/rpnet.2019.33.925

Chapter 3

Keywords: ESP, new technologies, teacher education, ZPTD.

1. Introduction

The aim of this research is to explore how ESP teachers and practitioners utilise new technologies, e.g. MOOCs, webinars, online platforms, etc. as a means of self-scaffolding in order to exceed their threshold in pedagogical, linguistic, and discoursal competencies in various ESP domains. Although scaffolding in teaching ESP has been vastly investigated (Hirvela, 2013; Luzón, 2007; Sinadinović, Mijomanović, & Aleksić-Hajduković, 2019; Sobhy, Berzosa, & Crean, 2013; Tzoannopoulou, 2015), the role of scaffolding in ESP teacher education has been largely undermined.

Furthermore, the role of technology in teaching and learning English for Specific Purposes has been widely discussed (Bloch, 2013; Franklin-Landi, 2017; Muñoz-Luna & Taillefer, 2018) as technology facilitates the incorporation of authentic audio-visual materials that meet the needs of (future) medical practitioners, economists, civil engineers, etc. However, this paper focuses on the role of new technologies in ESP teacher education and argues that it is no longer possible to neglect their pivotal role in the improvement of ESP teachers' teaching competence on their own and at their own pace.

Some previous works have indicated that technology has a positive impact on mediating the process of teacher learning. For instance, Lantolf (2004) describes technology, such as the Internet and computer along with associated software, as a dependable source of *electronic-scaffolding* which has acted as a mediator in their learning processes, while positively affecting the professional development of teachers. Therefore, one of the key questions posed is: how can ESP teachers utilise new technologies to further improve their teaching competence across various ESP domains? In this paper, *new technologies* pertain to software, apps, MOOCs, etc. (see Section 3, Figure 3) that can help ESP teachers upgrade their subject-specific knowledge and enhance their professional development. The paper attempts to provide some insights into this matter through the prism of the Vygotskyan notion of the Zone of Proximal Development (ZPD), which was later extrapolated to the Zone of Proximal Teacher Development (ZPTD) by Warford (2011) who used Sociocultural Theory (SCT) as a base.

According to Wood, Bruner, and Ross (1976), "the metaphor of scaffolding implies an educational concept in which a learner is equipped with tools and strategies that enable them to surpass their current developmental level and achieve goals within their range of competence" (p. 90). Integral to the notion of scaffolding is Vygotsky's (1978) theory of the ZPD, according to which "children's developmental potential is greatly improved through adult guidance and peer collaboration" (Santoso, 2010, pp. 47-48). Holton and Clarke (2006) state the following: "So for Vygotsky, a learner has an actual level of development and a potential for development. The difference between these two he called the zone of proximal development" (p. 128).

The conceptualisation of the ZPD and scaffolding provided by Holton and Clarke (2006), as opposed to *expert scaffolding* and *reciprocal scaffolding* that involve the aid of another person, i.e. the aid of an expert (e.g. a parent or a teacher) and a peer, respectively, *self-scaffolding* refers to an individual being in charge of their learning process in which they encounter new concepts and challenges.

Nonetheless, Warford (2011) argues that the ZPD could also be applied in the field of teacher education. As a result, the notion of the ZPTD has been explored by Warford (2011), who focuses on the distance between what teachers can do on their own and what they can achieve with the help of others (e.g. instructors, supervisors, etc.). Warford (2011) describes the ZPTD as "the distance between what teaching candidates can do on their own without assistance and a proximal level they might attain through strategically mediated assistance from more capable others (i.e. methods instructor or supervisor)" (p. 253). According to Warford (2011), there are four stages of the ZPTD: self- and teacher-assistance (Stages 1 and 2; initial), internalisation (Stage 3, advanced), and recurrence (Stage 4, advanced) (see Gallimore & Tharp, 1990; Warford, 2011).

Chapter 3

This chapter proposes that the stages of the ZPTD should be redefined as new technologies can now take on the role of a mediator, although they cannot replace teacher training courses/programmes. The present research shows that ESP teachers are eager to use new technologies to communicate and exchange ideas or examples of good practice. This is actually reciprocal scaffolding that proves that ESP teachers do not depend on new technologies solely, but they are also likely to rely on their fellow-teachers for further advancement and support. The method section provides further information on the research design, selection of research tools, participants' profiles, and a brief overview of data analysis.

2. Method

This research aims to explore how ESP teachers and practitioners utilise new technologies as a means of self-scaffolding in order to improve their competencies in various ESP domains. This study combining qualitative and quantitative approaches is based on a survey that consists of ten questions.

The survey was sent to various ESP teachers and practitioners coming from different countries and backgrounds. The survey, which was anonymous, was distributed in the virtual environment via ESP associations, organisations, and professional social media groups. A substantial number of participants worked in the business English domain (15). In the science, technology, engineering, and mathematics field there were 12 participants. There were eight participants in the domain of English for Medical Purposes and English for nurses, whereas seven participants deal with English for Academic Purposes. Apart from these, the following domains were represented in the survey: law (4), economics and management (3), education studies (2), maritime studies (2), English for Occupational Purposes (2), tourism (1), history (1), psychology (1), pharmacy (1), military studies (1), media (1), social sciences (1), agriculture (1), and applied arts (1).

Some of the participants worked in more than one field; therefore, all the responses were included. Some questions in the survey are open-ended, while others are closed-ended. Summative content analysis was conducted by deploying qualitative and quantitative data analysis. The first part dealt with general information concerning the ESP domain, educational level, country where the participants worked and their affiliation, as well as their years of experience. The second part examined the utilisation of new technologies in ESP education including honing competencies, new technology resources, strategies, and opportunities available for their unassisted professional development. There were 50 responses in total (N=50).

3. Results and discussion

This section provides the analysis of the research results concerning participants' structure, electronic self-scaffolding resources available to ESP teachers, and the way they exploit new technologies in self-directed professional development.

3.1. Participants' structure

When it comes to the educational level at which they teach, four participants provided more than one answer (i.e. tertiary/in-company; tertiary/adults; secondary/tertiary; and secondary/online). Most of the participants taught English at tertiary level (46), four participants worked at secondary level, two participants taught adults, one participant stated that they worked in-company, and one participant stated they worked online.

Table 1 shows the distribution of our participants across countries, i.e. where they teach. It can be noticed that teachers from 20 different countries took part in our survey while participants from Serbia, Poland, the US, and Russia were most represented. The majority of participants came from Europe, but teachers from four other continents participated as well.

Figure 1 illustrates how long the participants have been teaching in the field of ESP. It can be noticed that the majority of participants are highly experienced – 66% of all the participants have been teaching for between 11 and 31 years and there are only 8% of teachers who have been teaching for up to five years.

Chapter 3

Table 1. Countries where the participants teach

Country	Number (%)	Country	Number (%)
Serbia	14 (28%)	Mexico	1 (2%)
Poland	8 (16%)	Montenegro	1 (2%)
US	7 (14%)	Romania	1 (2%)
Russia	3 (6%)	Saudi Arabia	1 (2%)
Brazil	2 (4%)	Slovenia	1 (2%)
India	2 (4%)	Spain	1 (2%)
Algeria	1 (2%)	Switzerland	1 (2%)
Egypt	1 (2%)	Turkey	1 (2%)
Japan	1 (2%)	Ukraine	1 (2%)
Latvia	1 (2%)	Vietnam	1 (2%)

Figure 1. Experience in teaching ESP (number of years)

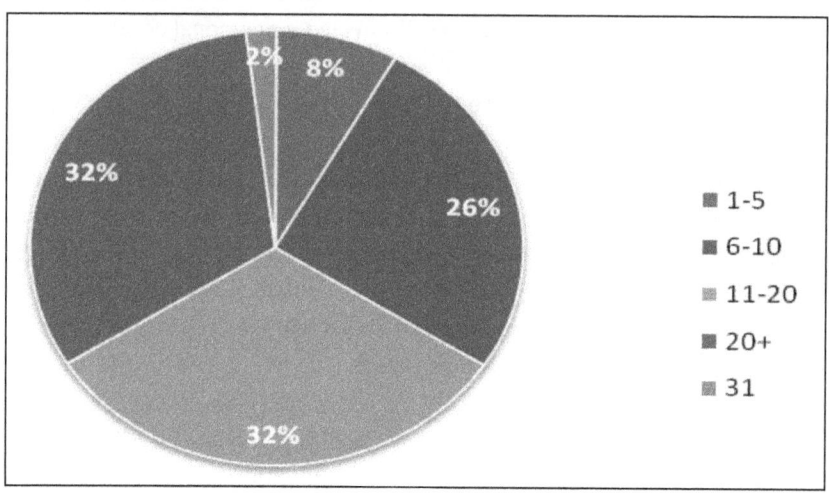

3.2. Self-scaffolding resources

Figure 2 shows in what context (private/public sector, institution/independent, etc.) our participants teach ESP. The results of the survey indicate that the majority of the participants teach at public universities (31). However, there is a significant number of those who are affiliated to private universities (14). Apart from public and private universities and schools, there are a few participants who teach at a workplace (i.e. companies) and very few teachers who are engaged in private tutoring or teaching online. For this question, the participants could provide more than one answer, which four of them did (secondary level/online lessons/tutoring; secondary level/primary; secondary level/college; and tertiary level/in-company).

Figure 2. The distribution of the respondents' affiliations

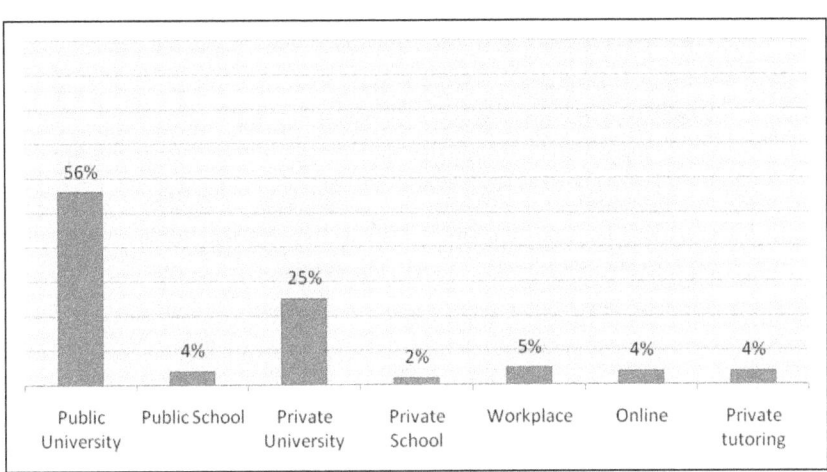

Table 2 shows to what extent the participants agree with the given statements designed to explore the reasons behind using new technologies. In this section, the participants were given five statements and evaluated each statement by choosing the answer they considered the most appropriate on a five-level Likert-type scale (1=I strongly disagree, 5=I entirely agree). Participants were asked if they used new technologies in order to: gain knowledge in their ESP domain (Statement 1); exchange ideas with other colleagues from their ESP domain (Statement 2); and improve their linguistic competences in their ESP domain (Statement 3). It was also checked whether they found new technologies that could improve their ESP teaching competencies to be easily accessible (Statement 4), and if it was easy to find out about new technologies that were compatible with their ESP domain (Statement 5). The answers to these questions were analysed using descriptive statistics, and our main focus was on the most positive and the most negative answers to every single question.

As can be seen from the answers to Statement 1, 46% of the participants believe they use new technologies for gaining knowledge in their ESP domain. Interestingly, none of the participants strongly disagreed with this statement, whereas 16% of them disagreed. Similarly, 34% of all the participants claim they use new technologies for exchanging ideas with their colleagues while only 6% of all the participants never seem to do that. Only 4% of all the participants believe they never use new technologies for improving their linguistic competencies in their ESP domain, whereas 38% of the participants think they definitely use new technologies to this purpose. So, analysing these three statements, it can be concluded that new technologies are used to a great extent and that the participants are well aware of them. The remaining two statements (Statement 4 and Statement 5) are predominantly evaluated using the most neutral value on Likert-type scale. Only 18% of all the participants entirely agree with the statement that new technologies that could improve their ESP teaching competencies are easily accessible, while only five participants (10%) entirely agree that it is easy to find out about new technologies they could use. So, it could be said that the participants in our research use new technologies to a rather great extent and that they do so to various purposes, but that they do not find particular new technologies accessible enough and easy to get informed about.

Table 2. Electronic self-scaffolding resources in ESP teacher education

STATEMENT	1	2	3	4	5
I use new technologies for gaining knowledge in my ESP domain.	0%	16%	18%	20%	46%
I use new technologies for exchanging ideas with other colleagues from my ESP domain.	6%	20%	20%	20%	34%
I use new technologies for improving my linguistic competences in my ESP domain.	4%	18%	16%	24%	38%
New technologies that could improve my ESP teaching competences are easily accessible.	6%	14%	40%	22%	18%
It is easy to find out about new technologies that are compatible with my ESP domain.	10%	14%	44%	22%	10%

3.3. New technologies in self-directed professional development of ESP teachers

When asked how they get informed about new technologies online, the participants stated it was mainly through professional development courses and professional communication. In the online category they listed searching/browsing the Internet (e.g. Google, Google Scholar), social and professional networks (e.g. Facebook, LinkedIn), specialist sites, and university websites. Professional development entails membership in professional organisations – e.g. Teaching English to Speakers of Other Languages (TESOL) –, webinars, MOOCs, attending courses, conferences, workshops, classes, and reading professional/vocational papers. Finally, when it comes to professional communication, what they particularly point out is professional exchange, followed by word of mouth (i.e. colleagues, students), online teaching communities, newsletters, and mailing lists.

Undoubtedly, our participants are quite eager when it comes to self-development and quite versatile in their approach to it. What is striking is the fact that they mostly rely on sources that either presuppose self-scaffolding or reciprocal scaffolding. However, most of the responses imply that they heavily rely on professional communication as a primary source of information.

Figure 3 demonstrates what new technologies the participants use for their self-directed professional development in their ESP domain. Online platforms (e.g. YouTube, TED-Ed, etc.) were obviously the most frequently chosen. These are followed by professional ESP websites, webinars, and social networks. Participants also made their own suggestions listing university online courses, educational websites aimed at professionals, and seminars for professional development.

The new technology resources that our participants listed as their favourite could be divided into 16 different categories: (1) publishers' websites and dictionaries, (2) online platforms, (3) online libraries, (4) webinars, (5) workshops, (6) file hosting services, (7) tools, (8) websites for e-learning/professional sites, (9) MOOCs, (10) e-books/online magazines, (11) professional associations' websites, (12) research engines, (13) discussion boards, (14) blogs, (15) podcasts, and (16) equipment.

Figure 3. New technologies used for self-directed professional development of ESP teachers

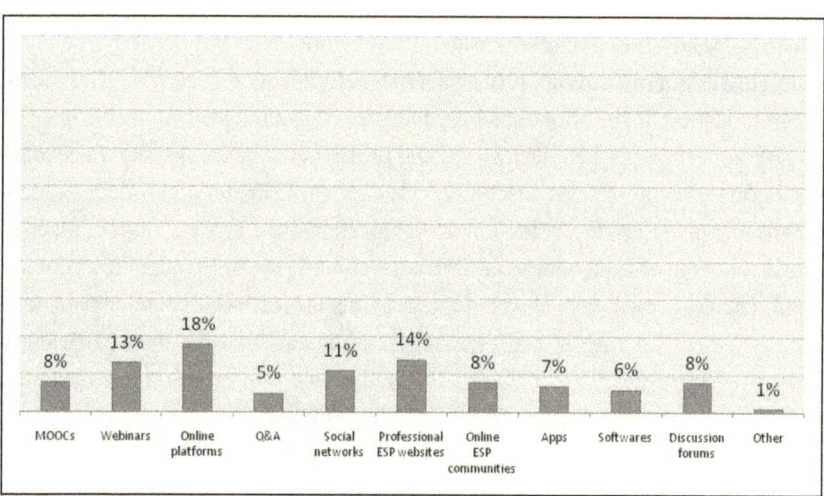

Oxford University Press, Pearson, and British Council resources were mentioned within Category 1, as well as free online dictionaries and online lexicons. Apart from the universally popular platforms such as YouTube and TED, the participants also mentioned platforms with instructional content including Newsela and Edmondo. JSTOR was listed as an example of an online library, while webinars hosted by Besingheim and Slovene Association of Language for Specific Purposes (LSP) Teachers were listed within Category 4. Electronic Village Online by TESOL was mentioned as an example of a workshop, whereas Dropbox and Google Drive represent Category 6. The participants were most elaborate regarding Category 7 as they listed MarEng (Maritime English tool), and the Windows photo story programme, besides the following apps: Quizlet, Kahoot, Pustulka.

The software the participants use include Powtoon, Turnitin, Infographics, Seagull software, ActivePresenter, Padlet, and language softwares, along with PowerPoint. KenHub, Cnet, open educational resources, ViDEOTEL, getnewsmart (business), history.com, studylegalenglish.com, become.

legalenglishexpert.pl, medical animation sites (e.g. xvivo), and Wikis were among those most mentioned in the category of websites for e-learning/ professional sites. The category of MOOCs was illustrated by Future Learn and Canvas, whereas ELTA, Consortium on Graduate Communication, and TESOL's ESP can be classified as professional associations' websites.

The mere number of the categories obtained by answering this question proves the importance and ubiquity of new technologies, not only for general teacher development, but for ESP teacher development. On the one hand, a considerable number of our participants still resort to the more traditional resources such as books and dictionaries even though these resources can now be found online in a format that fuses the old and the new. However, there is a predominance of fairly new inventions (e.g. MOOCs) that are being used as teaching tools and self-development tools at the same time. We can also observe that e-learning/ professional websites and online platforms represent common resources for improving one's teaching competencies in ESP. This might suggest a lack of formal courses or degrees that are specifically tailored for the existing variety of ESP teachers (e.g. Maritime English, Medical English, etc.).

Furthermore, the results suggest that ESP teachers might need additional skills and know-how in the future. The bulk of our participants use a variety of apps and software programmes, some of which require their users to be technologically savvy or to devote a fair amount of time to grasp the basic functions. Finally, the reliance on the professional community is evident, nevertheless, the arena is becoming increasingly virtual in nature.

Finally, when asked how they use new technologies to further develop their teaching competencies in their ESP domain, the participants provided answers that could be organised into five different categories: (1) self-study, (2) self-development, (3) information exchange, (4) classroom use, and (5) testing.

Regarding the self-study category, the participants use new technologies to find relevant literature as resources and references to be updated in their ESP domain, to deepen their knowledge of the domain, to read, learn new skills, watch videos and tutorials, and update and broaden their competencies in (business) terminology.

In the self-development category they use new technologies to access webinars (Oxford University Press), web conferences, discussion forums (TESOL), and professional ESP websites (TESOL) to get practice and experience, to develop their linguistic competencies, to search how to use new technologies, to apply professional programmes in expanding their specialist knowledge, to learn new skills, for continual professional development, to acquire the latest pedagogical tools to improve their teaching, and to update and broaden their competencies in business terminology.

For information exchange, our participants use new technologies to share information with students/colleagues, for professional exchange, to access news feeds from social network groups and discussion forums (TESOL). The participants use new technologies in the classroom to access/find relevant material e.g. videos, as source material for lessons/course development, for development of their students' linguistic competencies, to search for activities that can be used with students, to assign tasks, to introduce new approaches for teaching 'old' things (e.g. using an interactive whiteboard), for using videos in the classroom (e.g. pronunciation drill), for development of activities based on video content, for recording micro teaching sessions and their discussion and evaluation with students, and for skills development.

Finally, for testing, our participants use new technologies to develop their own web based applications for ESP.

The participants also use online platforms, MOOCs, apps, and online courses. All of these are used for self-study and self-development. Online platforms, MOOCs, and apps are used in the classroom, and online platforms and apps are used for information exchange and testing.

As regards self-study, we can see that the emphasis is placed on obtaining new information and deepening the knowledge within a particular domain, while the self-development category adds honing both linguistic and non-linguistic skills including pedagogical and technological skills, as well as the acquisition of new tools. Even though the third category is self-explanatory, it is evident that new technologies are used as an easier and faster way of communication with students and with the professional community. The fourth category shows us how new technologies are used for finding materials and activities for class use, for honing skills, course development, and for developing student's linguistic competencies. Finally, not only do our participants use new technologies for the purpose of testing, but they also take part in developing them. It is interesting to note that a few of these appear in almost every category. For instance, online platforms and apps are included in all the categories, whereas MOOCs are mentioned in three (self-study, self-development, and classroom use), and online courses in two (self-study and self-development). Another important fact is that there are these five groups in particular, rather than some other combination. Therefore, we propose that new technologies actually serve as electronic-scaffolding (*e-scaffolding*) that can be further broken down into self-scaffolding (self-study and self-development), reciprocal scaffolding (information exchange), and as a source of pedagogical tools.

4. Conclusions

This research has provided ample evidence of how ESP teachers and practitioners utilise new technologies. ESP teachers have demonstrated an insatiable need to enhance their teaching competencies by turning to new technologies (i.e. MOOCs, software, apps, etc.). The research has shown that ESP teachers use new technologies to a rather great extent and that they do so for various purposes, even though they do not always find them easily accessible or simple to use.

Furthermore, the data indicate that e-learning/professional websites and online platforms represent common resources for improving one's teaching competencies in ESP. This might suggest a lack of formal courses or degrees that are specifically tailored for the existing variety of ESP teachers.

Most importantly, this research highlights the need to redefine the outdated model of the ZPTD by acknowledging *e-scaffolding* as the fifth stage of the ZPTD that co-exists with the other four stages defined in the 1990s when the new technologies had just started to emerge.

Offering an up-to-date model for ESP teacher education is an important implication of this research whose findings could serve as guidelines and contribute to materials development.

Finally, the limitations of this research are cross-cultural differences in ESP teacher education, which are beyond the scope of the research. Nevertheless, this paper provides a universal representation of current trends in ESP teacher education and the role of new technologies in unassisted professional development of ESP teachers. Further research is well-advised in order to explore field specific nuances, cultural differences, and (in)accessibility to new technologies investigated in the paper, including financial and institutional aspects.

Acknowledgements

We would like to thank the following LSP and ESP teacher associations and their members for taking part in the research: EALTHY, ELTA Serbia, IESPTA, TESOL, and Foreign Language and Literature Association of Serbia with its LSP special interest group.

References

Bloch, J. (2013). Technology and ESP. In B. Paltridge & S. Starfield (Eds), *The handbook of English for specific purposes* (pp. 385-401). John Wiley & Sons.

Franklin-Landi, R. (2017). Identifying and responding to learner needs at the medical faculty: the use of audio-visual specialised fiction (FASP). In C. Sarré & S. Whyte (Eds), *New developments in ESP teaching and learning research* (pp. 153-170). Research-publishing.net. https://doi.org/10.14705/rpnet.2017.cssw2017.750

Gallimore, R., & Tharp, R. (1990). Teaching mind in society: teaching, schooling, and literate discourse. In L. Moll (Ed.), *Vygotsky and education: instructional implications and applications of sociohistorical psychology* (pp. 175-205). Cambridge University Press. https://doi.org/10.1017/cbo9781139173674.009

Hirvela, A. (2013). ESP and Reading. In B. Paltridge & S. Starfield (Eds), *The handbook of English for specific purposes* (pp. 77-94). John Wiley & Sons. https://doi.org/10.1002/9781118339855.ch4

Holton, D., & Clarke, D. (2006). Scaffolding and metacognition. *International Journal of Mathematical Education in Science and Technology, 37*(2), 127-143. https://doi.org/10.1080/00207390500285818

Lantolf, J. P. (2004). Overview of sociocultural theory. In O. S. John, K. van Esch & E. Schalkwijk (Eds), *New insights in second language learning and teaching* (pp. 13-34). Peter Lang Verlag.

Luzón, M. J. (2007). Enhancing WebQuest for effective ESP learning. *CORELL: Computer resources for language learning, 1*, 1-13. https://www.ucam.edu/sites/default/files/corell/MJLuzon.pdf

Muñoz-Luna, R., & Taillefer, L. (Eds). (2018). *Integrating information and communication technologies in English for specific purposes*. Springer International Publishing. https://doi.org/10.1007/978-3-319-68926-5

Santoso, A. (2010). *Scaffolding an EFL (English as a foreign language) 'effective writing' class in a hybrid learning community*. Doctoral dissertation. Queensland University of Technology.

Sinadinović, D., Mijomanović S., & Aleksić-Hajduković, I. (2019). Instructional scaffolding in English for Medical Purposes: towards enhancing a student-centred approach in large classes. In *Proceedings from LSP '18: The Third International Conference from Theory to Practice in Language for Specific Purposes*. Association of LSP Teachers at Higher Education Institutions.

Sobhy, N. N., Berzosa, C., & Crean, F. (2013). From ESP to CLIL using the schema theory. *LFE: Revista de lenguas para fines específicos, 19*, 261-278.

Tzoannopoulou, M. (2015). Rethinking ESP: integrating content and language in the university classroom. *Procedia-Social and Behavioral Sciences, 173*, 149-153. https://doi.org/10.1016/j.sbspro.2015.02.045

Vygotsky, L. (1978). Interaction between learning and development. *Readings on the development of children, 23*(3), 34-41.

Chapter 3

Warford, M. (2011). The zone of proximal teacher development. *Teaching and Teacher Education, 27*(2), 252-258. https://doi.org/10.1016/j.tate.2010.08.008

Wood, D., Bruner, J. S., & Ross, G. (1976). The role of tutoring in problem solving. *Journal of child psychology and psychiatry, 17*(2), 89-100. https://doi.org/10.1111/j.1469-7610.1976.tb00381.x

4 Providing feedback on the lexical use of ESP students' academic presentations: teacher training considerations

Alla Zareva[1]

Abstract

This chapter offers a description of a methodology for providing training to pre-service English for Academic and Specific Purposes (EAP/ESP) teacher trainees in giving evidence-based feedback on the lexical composition of ESP students' academic presentations. It also discusses a study based on the analysis of the mock feedback provided by the EAP/ESP teacher trainees ($n=20$) to ESP students' presentations with a focus on the effects of training. The results revealed that the training was successful in areas such as raising the teacher trainees' awareness of how to evaluate various lexical categories in an ESP presentation, how to incorporate their evaluation into the feedback they give to the students, how to highlight relevant lexical deviations in an evidence-based manner, etc. There were, however, a couple of areas that needed to be emphasised more in the training process. The results confirmed that providing training on evidence-driven feedback to teacher trainees planning to teach in an EAP/ESP context is a necessary component of ESP teacher education.

Keywords: ESP teacher training, lexical composition, ESP presentation analysis, data-based feedback.

1. Old Dominion University, Norfolk, Virginia, United States; azareva@odu.edu

How to cite this chapter: Zareva, A. (2019). Providing feedback on the lexical use of ESP students' academic presentations: teacher training considerations. In S. Papadima-Sophocleous, E. Kakoulli Constantinou & C. N. Giannikas (Eds), *ESP teaching and teacher education: current theories and practices* (pp. 63-78). Research-publishing.net. https://doi.org/10.14705/rpnet.2019.33.926

Chapter 4

1. Introduction

Higher education has never been as internationalised as we know it today. The number of international students worldwide has increased by 99% in the 2000-2010 period with Europe being the preferred destination for 41% of international students (Immigration of international students to the EU, 2012). Similarly, the international enrollments at the highest levels of education – Master's (MA) and doctoral level programmes – have also significantly increased, and countries like the United States, United Kingdom, Australia, Canada, etc. host the largest proportion of international students at those degree levels (Education at a glance, 2017). Thus, higher education, especially at a graduate level, has started to demand solid ESP knowledge more than ever before so that the international students attending English-based graduate programmes can successfully put their disciplinary expertise on display from the start.

At the same time, ESP teacher training as a focus of interest and research is lagging behind other areas, such as ESP material design, needs analysis, the role of specialised knowledge, classroom discourse, etc. (Basturkmen, 2014; Coxhead, 2013; Hall, 2013; Kennedy, 1983). More than 35 years ago, Kennedy (1983) rightfully pointed out what is still true today – i.e. that one area which has received little attention in language for specific purposes is the desirability of providing ESP training to Teaching English to Speakers of Other Languages (TESOL) teachers. Few MA TESOL programmes offer ESP specialisation in some of their classes and even fewer offer courses on ESP (Belcher, 2013) which, consequently, leads to having underprepared teachers entering ESP classrooms. At the very least, MA TESOL programmes should include in their coursework discussions that examine different aspects of each of the components of the ESP acronym itself (Hall, 2013) – i.e. analysis of the *English* language, its *specificity* in various contexts of use, and the professional and disciplinary *purposes* it can be used for.

This chapter will offer a description of a methodology for providing training to graduate students preparing to be TESOL or EAP/ESP teachers on how to give evidence-based feedback on the lexical composition of ESP students' academic presentations. In what follows, I will first discuss the notion of *Assessment for Learning* (AfL) with a focus on constructive lexical feedback that pre-experience and pre-service EAP/ESP teacher trainees need to learn how to provide so that they can be relevant to the discipline-specific language needs of their ESP students. Second, I will elaborate on the notions of lexical levels and lexical complexity as important features of the lexicon in use for subject-specific purposes. Finally, I will discuss the findings of a qualitative study which looked at the effects of training on developing EAP/ESP teachers' awareness of how to provide constructive evidence-driven lexical feedback on ESP students' academic presentations.

1.1. The central role of feedback in the assessment for learning approach

In recent years, there has been a worldwide movement in general education towards AfL as a form of assessment that integrates teaching, learning, and assessment holistically (Cheng, 2013; Mumm, Karm, & Remmik, 2016). Along the same lines, Sambell, McDowell, and Montgomery (2013) have pointed out that AfL involves six main practices, i.e. (1) designing authentic assessment assignments linked to acquiring skills and knowledge that the professional field expects, (2) balancing AfL and summative assessment, (3) creating opportunities for practice before assessing summatively, (4) providing timely feedback to improve learning, (5) designing opportunities for feedback as part of the learning process, and (6) developing opportunities for students to assess their own progress.

Recently, various studies have confirmed that AfL should be seen as a broad approach in which all these practices contribute to learning; however, they also indicate that feedback can be considered the most impactful one (Cheng, 2013; Mumm et al., 2016; Sambell, et al., 2013). Equally importantly, central to the notion of AfL is that feedback should make students understand the learning task better so that they can effectively improve their own performance. Thus, it should be clear, encouraging, consistent with the assignment, and with a focus on key errors and areas for improvement (Cheng, 2013, p. 28). Fisher and Frey

Chapter 4

(2009) further identified three distinct components of feedback that need to be fully implemented for the feedback to be effective: *feed up*, *feedback*, and *feed forward*. In *feed up*, the authors recommended that teachers should articulate clearly the learning goals for their students so that they know where to focus their learning efforts; in *feedback*, teachers should provide descriptive feedback that targets the learning goals; and *feed forward* goes back to teaching and should inform instructional modifications.

As much as these practices are relevant to general education, they are also equally relevant to EAP/ESP teacher preparation primarily because EAP/ESP teachers in training need to be able to address the general language learning needs of ESP students in addition to their language-specific growth. In this regard, it becomes particularly important to offer specific training to EAP/ESP teacher trainees in how to provide constructive feedback to ESP students that addresses both their use of discipline-specific language as well as general language areas. Needless to say, the first step in this endeavour should be to make the teacher trainees aware of what counts as language features that are specific to a field or discipline and what does not. In the context of this study, the focus of the training was on distinguishing the various levels of vocabulary description and features of lexical complexity and providing evidence-driven feedback on the ones that enhance the quality of ESP academic presentations.

1.2. Aspects of the lexicon EAP/ESP teacher trainees need to be aware of

Discussions of various aspects of teaching, learning, and feedback on vocabulary knowledge in speaking and writing should be one of the central topics in EAP/ESP teacher training coursework. One of the well-established distinctions in the description of vocabulary for EAP/ESP purposes is Nation's (2001) distinction of four main lexical levels, i.e. (1) high frequency words, which include the first 2,000 most frequent words of English (e.g. *give, language, usually*), (2) academic vocabulary, which includes the 570 word family Academic Word List (AWL) identified by Coxhead (2000) (e.g. *research, academic, virtually*), (3) technical/specialised vocabulary, which is the bulk of vocabulary that is discipline- or subject-area-specific (e.g. *vocabulary, morpheme, syntax*), and (4) low frequency words, which cover the vocabulary beyond the other three levels.

Recommendations concerning the importance of the lexicon for academic and specific purposes commonly highlight several points in relation to the four-level distinction of the lexicon. A point of unanimous agreement is that the 2,000 most frequent words of English provide the greatest coverage of vocabulary used in academic and non-academic texts (e.g. Morris & Cobb, 2004; Nation, 2001; Zareva, 2012, 2019, forthcoming). However, in academic and specialised contexts, the importance of the three levels beyond the 2,000 words (i.e. AWL, technical/specialised, and lower frequency vocabulary) greatly increases, as it is those lexical layers that allow proficient EAP/ESP users to put their academic and disciplinary knowledge on display in a relevant way (Nation, 2001; Zareva, forthcoming). There is also a growing realisation among teachers and ESP learners that those same layers bring lexical richness to students' disciplinary writing and/or speaking and enhance their ability to fare well in their disciplinary studies and, later on, in professional contexts.

The notion of lexical richness (Read, 2000) or lexical complexity (Bulté & Housen, 2012) is closely linked to the four-level description of the lexicon and fundamentally based on the distinction between what counts as simple and what counts as complex lexical use. For EAP/ESP teachers in training, the key to understanding this distinction is not only to become aware of what the basic words are (i.e. the first 2,000 most common English words) and what the sophisticated ones are (i.e. AWL, technical/specialised, and lower frequency vocabulary), but also to become cognisant of the fact that they contribute differently to the lexical complexity of ESP users' performances. That is, the first 2,000 words account for anywhere between 90% of the vocabulary in conversations to about 78% in written academic texts (Nation, 2001), which confirms their primary importance across the registers. However, what sets the EAP/ESP register apart from the less formal and specialised ones lexically is the increased use of vocabulary from the academic, technical/specialised, and lower frequency levels that, altogether, bring disciplinary precision and appropriateness to the discourse. As Coxhead (2013) pointed out, when such knowledge of vocabulary is put into use, it enhances the impression of fluency and helps "second language speakers sound as though they belong to a community of language users who make meaning through using the same vocabulary in specific ways" (p. 2).

The models of lexical richness or complexity identify, at least, three dimensions of lexical complexity – i.e. lexical sophistication, lexical density, and lexical diversity. In this regard, EAP/ESP teachers in training need to understand that, on the one hand, the three dimensions (lexical sophistication, density, and diversity) are relatively independent, which means that teachers need to work with their students on each one of them separately. On the other hand, they also need to know that the dimensions can be captured by different measures, which can help them provide evidence-based feedback to EAP/ESP students' vocabulary use (for a detailed description of the dimensions, see Bulté & Housen, 2012; Read, 2000; Zareva, 2012, 2019, forthcoming). In brief, the lexically sophisticated texts will have a higher proportion of lower frequency words which, along with the uncommon lower frequency words, will also include the jargon, technical, and subject-specific vocabulary. The more lexically dense texts will have a higher ratio of content words (nouns, verbs, adjectives, and adverbs) as they are linked to more informationally packed messages. Finally, the more lexically diverse texts will have a greater number of different words (vs. a limited number of words used repetitively) and the simplest (though not uncontroversial) way to capture lexical diversity is by the Type–Token Ratio (TTR).

1.3. Main objectives of the study

A preliminary in-class discussion of the lexical features of academic ESP presentations in terms of what they are, how they can be included in the feedback, and how the feedback can move from impressionistic to evidence-based revealed that the participating EAP/ESP teacher trainees had a vague idea about how to address these questions and a little sense of how to approach the task of feedback. Thus, the training the students received (described in greater detail in the next section) had to provide them with the necessary background knowledge of the various lexical features (e.g. vocabulary description levels, lexical complexity, etc.), their realisation in EAP/ESP speech, as well as how to approach the task at hand.

The study discussed below offers a description of a training methodology in this regard. It is qualitative and exploratory in nature and aimed at finding more about the effects of training on developing EAP/ESP teacher trainees' awareness of giving feedback on various aspects of vocabulary and lexical complexity. The discussion of the findings is based on the analysis of the participants' mock feedback given on ESP presentations, which was a graded assignment in a TESOL course the teacher trainees were taking at the time of the experiment. The findings will be discussed with respect to their implications for EAP/ESP teacher training coursework provided in many TESOL programmes.

2. Method

2.1. Participants and data

The participating EAP/ESP teacher trainees ($N=20$, $n=17$ females, and $n=3$ males) were English-speaking college students at a US university. At the time of data collection, they were taking courses in completion of their MA degrees either in applied linguistics or education with a concentration in TESOL. The participants reported they considered it important to have good presentation skills ($M=5.4$ on a six-point scale) and 65% of them ($n=13$) also self-reported to have had previous formal training in giving presentations as part of their required undergraduate coursework in public speaking and communication. However, none of them reported having had previous experience in teaching or giving feedback to ESP presentations.

The ESP presenters ($N=20$, $n=9$ females, and $n=11$ males), whose presentations were analysed and given feedback on, were also college students. They were enrolled in various programmes and disciplinary areas such as economics, environmental studies, journalism, computer sciences, health sciences, and applied linguistics. Their presentations were given to satisfy some course requirement in their respective programme of study. They were native (L1) speakers of 13 languages (e.g. Arabic, Chinese, French, German, Hindi, Polish, Russian, Spanish, etc.). The ESP presenters reported having studied English through formal instruction in their native countries and no instruction or training in giving a presentation before. Their proficiency scores placed them in the category of higher proficiency users.

The presentations were audio-recorded at the time of delivery, transcribed orthographically by the EAP/ESP teacher trainees, and then analysed by them in several ways. The training procedure is described in the next section.

2.2. Training procedure

At the time of data collection, the participating EAP/ESP teacher trainees were taking a course in TESOL Methods and Materials which included a component on EAP/ESP teaching, assessment, and evidence-based feedback on ESP academic presentations. Few of the course participants had prior experience in teaching EAP or ESP; however, most of them expected to teach in such contexts in the future. One of the graded course assignments in this class was for the teacher trainees to transcribe an ESP presentation, analyse it, and provide written mock feedback to the student-presenter with a focus on vocabulary. Below is a step-by-step description of the training the EAP/ESP teacher trainees received before they started working on the assignment.

First, the teacher trainees were assigned a reading on AfL and feedback (in this case, Cheng, 2013), which was discussed in class both in general terms and with respect to its relevance to ESP teaching.

Next, they read an article (in this case, Zareva, 2012) which looked at the lexical composition of effective student academic presentations and introduced a user-friendly procedure for determining their lexical features and complexity. Later on, they used the study as an aid in evaluating the ESP students' presentations they analysed and determining if they fell within the established baselines of the various categories. The article was discussed in class in terms of:

- the various levels of vocabulary description (e.g. the contribution of the first 2,000 most common English words, AWL, technical/specialised vocabulary, other lower frequency vocabulary, and various disfluencies that typically occur in student presentations);

- what a typical lexical distribution of a successful academic presentation looks like;

- the notion of lexical complexity with an emphasis on the role of academic, technical/specialised, and lower frequency vocabulary;

- the procedure and measurements that can be used to analyse the lexical composition of texts for the purpose of providing evidence-driven feedback;

- how to interpret the percentage distributions of the various lexical categories, especially the noticeable deviations from the baselines;

- how to incorporate the data interpretations into the presentations' feedback provided to the ESP students.

Following the discussion of the article, the EAP/ESP teacher trainees were given audio files of ESP presentations, accompanied by their PowerPoints, and were asked to transcribe them orthographically. The goal of this task was to give them the experience of working with ESP oral data and the opportunity to get to know the presentations they were going to analyse and give feedback on intimately. The transcription task was also aimed at raising the teacher trainees' awareness of various language features beyond the content of the presentation.

The next step was to introduce the teacher trainees to a free online vocabulary profiling programme called Compleat Lexical Tutor (Cobb, 2002: http://www.lextutor.ca/) by demonstrating how the programme works and providing an additional explanation of the categories included in the output (e.g. the TTR, lexical density, lexical diversity, etc.). The students were recommended to use the classical version of the programme for this assignment. This step ensured that the teacher trainees could reliably interpret the quantitative output of the analysed presentations before writing up their feedback.

Finally, the teacher trainees were given some suggestions about writing up their analysis and mock feedback. Even though feedback to oral discourse is usually given orally, the goal of the task was to make the EAP/ESP teacher trainees consciously aware of how to shape their feedback so that it captured the quantified lexical composition of their analysis, highlighted the areas of success and the ones that needed improvement, and should become a stepping stone for learning. The suggestions included a greater variety of language features that could be given feedback on; however, the focus of this study will be only on the lexical features that the student trainees commented on in their mock feedback.

3. Results and discussion

Giving an effective presentation of specialised material is one of the most daunting tasks for EAP/ESP students for a variety of reasons some of which may relate to anxiety, lack of previous experience in giving presentations, L2 insecurities, and lack of knowledge of the disciplinary conventions regarding the genre, etc. It also turned out to be an equally daunting task for the EAP/ESP teacher trainees in this study to give constructive feedback to such presentations without the specific training they received. Overall, the training resulted in noticeable gains in the quality of their feedback on the lexical features of the ESP presentations they analysed. In what follows, I am going to discuss briefly the patterns that could be determined in the teacher trainees' mock feedback as a result of the training with an eye on the areas of achievement and the ones that are in need of improvement.

Relating the lexical comments that the teacher trainees incorporated in their written mock feedback to Cheng's (2013) recommendations about high quality feedback, the analysis uncovered four main patterns that emerged as a result of the training, which are discussed below.

3.1. Discussion of the distribution of the various lexical levels provided by the vocabulary profiling programme (provided by 100% of the EAP/ESP teacher trainees)

The finding that all participating EAP/ESP teacher trainees included in their mock feedback a discussion of the distribution of the four levels of vocabulary in the presentations (basic, AWL, technical/specialised, and low frequency vocabulary) and the various dimensions of lexical complexity (lexical sophistication, diversity, and density) revealed that they all utilised the Vocab Profiler programme in their analysis. The Vocab Profiler output shows the numerical values of a number of lexical features, which the teacher trainees not only interpreted skillfully in relation to the baselines discussed in Zareva's (2012) article, but also explained to the ESP students their value and contribution to the effectiveness of a presentation. Thus, with their feedback, the teacher trainees were able to accomplish simultaneously several important tasks – i.e. educate the ESP students about the contribution of the different vocabulary levels, put their presentations in the broader context of what typically a good vocabulary profile in academic speaking looks like, and later on comment and/or give lexical recommendations for improvement. Thus, the training seemed to raise not only the teacher trainees' awareness of the value of the lexicon in ESP context, but also prompt them to raise their students' awareness of how the various lexical features work together in the presentation as a specific genre.

3.2. Evidence-based critical comments to the presenters' lexical use (provided by 95% of the EAP/ESP trainees)

As a result of transcribing the presentations and running them through the Vocab Profiler, the teacher trainees were able to identify specific instances and patterns of lexical misuses that otherwise could easily go unnoticed. In their lexical feedback, 95% of the trainees addressed and gave examples of lexical mispronunciations, lexical misuses (e.g. "Your vocabulary choices were good but there were some words that are not real English words such as the word 'credibilize'"), unstable collocations (e.g. "You consistently used the term *fossil energy* to refer to 'fossil fuels'"), the use of 'false friends' (e.g. "You rely heavily

Chapter 4

on the strategy of substituting an unknown word with a false friend word; however, this backfires in the case of your using the word *cart*, for example, to refer to 'a map' (L1 German *Karte)*").

Some of the comments also pointed out instances of much higher rates than typical of truncated words, repetitions, false starts, and disfluencies (e.g. the use of too many inserts, 'uhms' and 'uhs', overuse of 'so' as a transition choice between slides, etc.) and added an explanation of the impression those may create in a listener. Some teacher trainees also commented on the deviations from the baseline in the lexical complexity of some presentations or when the use of academic, technical/specialised, and lower frequency vocabulary was markedly lower than the expected average. All in all, these comments seemed to confirm the positive effect the training had on the teacher trainees' ability to notice and highlight relevant lexical deviations in an evidence-based manner.

3.3. Positive comments about various aspects of vocabulary use in the presentations (provided by 40% of the EAP/ESP teachers)

A relatively small number (n=8) of the EAP/ESP teacher trainees included positive comments in their written feedback which shows that this is an area that needs to be addressed more consistently in teacher training, especially in relation to feedback. The value of feedback lies as much in the constructive criticism as it does in the acknowledgement of the accomplishments. The EAP/ESP teacher trainees who acknowledged the lexical accomplishments of the ESP presenters highlighted their "stable vocab choices across all categories", "the impressive use of specialised and academic vocab", the high incidence of content specific words that were beyond the AWL words, the infrequent use of phrasal verbs which revealed a "generally more formal presentation style", "the smooth and well managed transitions", "the small number of fillers", and praised the performances which showed similar lexical distributions to the baselines.

One plausible explanation of the relatively low incidence of positive comments in the teacher trainees' mock feedback is that it is highly possible that they saw the main purpose of the feedback primarily in providing negative/corrective language feedback to the ESP students. However, while negative/corrective feedback is a necessary part of language learning, it is usually the positive feedback that keeps learners motivated (Cheng, 2013). In that sense, it seems that the training provided to the teacher trainees fell short of emphasising the importance of this aspect of the feedback strongly enough for the participants to incorporate it consistently in their feedback.

3.4. Lexical recommendations (included by 30% of the EAP/ESP teachers)

Even a smaller number of teacher trainees attempted to give advice and recommendations for lexical improvements in their mock feedback. The majority of these recommendations (70%) were about the use of fillers and concerned strategies the ESP students could use to avoid their excessive use. Only a small number of recommendations were specifically directed to setting vocabulary improvement goals, which suggests that the link between the critical comments to the ESP presenters' lexical use and setting up vocabulary improvement goals in the feedback was not as obvious to the majority of the teacher trainees as assumed. In this regard, future training should, perhaps, clearly spell out the important connection that should be made in language feedback between critical remarks concerning areas of errors and recommendations about how to improve those areas.

4. Conclusions

The study was an attempt to find out more about the effects of training on developing pre-experience TESOL teachers' awareness of how to provide evidence-based feedback on the lexical usage of ESP students' presentations. The training was designed around the framework of the AfL approach, which emphasises values such as using for assessment purposes assignments that the professional world of the learner requires, providing clear, evidence-based feedback that helps the learner understand the learning task better and sets for them improvement goals, etc. – values that ESP teacher education also cherishes and tries to incorporate in their coursework.

Providing feedback is not intuitive to pre-service student teachers, and the teacher trainees participating in this study were no exception to the rule. The training they received seemed to be successful in some respects and lacking in others. It was successful in raising the teacher trainees' awareness of how to evaluate various lexical categories in an ESP presentation; how to incorporate their evaluation into the mock feedback they gave to the ESP students; how to make the lexical feedback evidence-based; how to highlight relevant lexical deviations in an evidence-based manner; and how to raise the ESP learners' awareness of the way different lexical features work together in an effective presentation.

Two areas that seemed to need to be more explicitly emphasised in the training process were areas that the majority of the teacher trainees failed to account for in their mock feedback – i.e. to include positive comments on the ESP students' lexical accomplishments and to connect their critical comments to clear recommendations about areas in need of improvement. On a final note, the present study was a small scale exploratory study with some limitations (for instance, small number of participating teacher trainees, little diversity in the proficiency level of the ESP presenters, teacher trainees' feedback was analysed only qualitatively, etc.); however, it confirmed that providing ESP training to TESOL teachers planning to teach in EAP/ESP contexts is more than a strong recommendation. It is a must.

References

Basturkmen, H. (2014). LSP teacher education: review of literature and suggestions for the research agenda. *Ibérica, 28*, 17-34.
Belcher, D. (2013). The future of ESP research: resources for access and choice. In B. Paltridge & S. Starfield (Eds), *The handbook of English for specific purposes* (pp. 535-551). John Wiley & Sons. https://doi.org/10.1002/9781118339855.ch28

Bulté, B., & A. Housen, A. (2012). Defining and operationalising L2 complexity. In A. Housen, F. Kuiken & I. Vedder (Eds), *Dimensions of L2 performance and proficiency: complexity, accuracy and fluency in SLA* (pp. 21-46). John Benjamins. https://doi.org/10.1075/lllt.32.02bul

Cheng, L. (2013). *Language classroom assessment.* TESOL International Association.

Cobb, T. (2002). *Web VocabProfile* (v. 3 Classic). http://www.lextutor.ca/vp/eng/

Coxhead, A. (2000). A new academic word list. *TESOL Quarterly, 34*(2), 213-238. https://doi.org/10.2307/3587951

Coxhead, A. (2013). Vocabulary and language for specific purposes. In C. A. Chapelle (Ed.), *The encyclopedia of applied linguistics.* Blackwell. https://doi.org/10.1002/9781405198431.wbeal1266

Education at a Glance. (2017). *Centre for educational research and innovation.* https://www.oecd-ilibrary.org/education/education-at-a-glance-2017_eag-2017-en

Fisher, D., & Frey, N. (2009). Feed up, back, forward. *Educational Leadership, 67*(3), 20-25.

Hall. D. (2013). Teacher education for language for specific purposes. In C. A. Chapelle (Ed.), *The encyclopedia of applied linguistics.* Blackwell. https://doi.org/10.1002/9781405198431.wbeal1144

Immigration of international students to the EU. (2012). *European migration network study.* http://emn.ie/cat_publication_detail.jsp?clog=1&itemID=2547&t=6

Kennedy, C. (1983). An ESP approach to EFL/ESL teacher training. *ESP Journal, 2*(1), 73-85. https://doi.org/10.1016/0272-2380(83)90024-0

Morris, L., & Cobb, T. (2004). Vocabulary profiles as predictors of the academic performance of teaching English as a second language trainees. *System, 32*, 75-87. https://doi.org/10.1016/j.system.2003.05.001

Mumm, K., Karm, M., & Remmik, M. (2016). Assessment for learning: why assessment does not always support student teachers' learning. *Journal of Further and Higher Education, 40*(6), 780-803. http://dx.doi.org/10.1080/0309877X.2015.1062847

Nation, I. S. P. (2001). *Learning vocabulary in another language.* Cambridge University Press.

Read, J. (2000). *Assessing vocabulary.* Cambridge University Press.

Sambell, K., McDowell, L., & Montgomery, C. (2013). *Assessment for learning in higher education.* Routledge.

Zareva, A. (2012). Lexical composition of effective L1 and L2 student academic presentations. *Journal of Applied Linguistics, 6*(1), 91-110. https://doi.org/10.1558/japl.v6i1.91

Chapter 4

Zareva, A. (2019). Lexical complexity of academic presentations: similarities despite situational differences. *Journal of Second Language Studies, 2*(1), 72-93.

Zareva, A. (forthcoming). Setting the lexical EAP bar for ESL learners: lexical complexity of L2 academic presentations. In P. Ecke & S. Rott (Eds), *Understanding vocabulary learning and teaching: implications for language program development.* American Association of University Supervisors, Coordinators, and Directors of Language Programs.

5. Validating new perspectives and methodologies for learning and teacher training in English for aeronautical communications

Neil Bullock[1]

Abstract

English for Specific Purposes (ESP) is often governed by pre-defined communicative functions and rules within a specific domain. Radio communication between pilots and Air Traffic Controllers (ATCOs) is one such domain. Mandatory plain language testing, introduced in this domain in 2008, whilst clearly laudable in its safety related objectives, has often resulted in language being seen, and taught, in isolation, creating a disconnect between the classroom and the real-world. In 2015, Bullock argued for a change of perspectives in Language For Specific Purposes (LSP) teaching towards a methodology that would adopt a more inclusive communication and knowledge-based approach. Three years later, with evidence that the aforementioned disconnect remained, a pilot study was conducted with 33 student ATCOs to demonstrate how a more appropriate methodology could transfer such theory into practice and address real-world communication needs. This article discusses the research results, and demonstrates the positive learning impact such methodology had on the students. It suggests integrating this into more appropriate training for LSP teachers, offering learners a more appropriate environment in which to maintain and improve communication skills through language.

1. English Plus LTS, Concise, Switzerland; neilbullock@englishplus.ch

How to cite this chapter: Bullock, N. (2019). Validating new perspectives and methodologies for learning and teacher training in English for aeronautical communications. In S. Papadima-Sophocleous, E. Kakoulli Constantinou & C. N. Giannikas (Eds), *ESP teaching and teacher education: current theories and practices* (pp. 79-93). Research-publishing.net. https://doi.org/10.14705/rpnet.2019.33.927

Chapter 5

Keywords: specific purpose, aviation English, aeronautical communication, phraseology, communicative competence.

1. Introduction

Dialogue in aeronautical communication between pilots and ATCOs relies principally on speaking and listening skills via the radiotelephone – International Civil Aviation Organisation (ICAO, 2010). In routine operations, such interaction is covered by internationally agreed standard phraseology – a fixed and restricted code of single lexical items (*roger, negative, wilco,* etc.) and short directly referential phrases (*say again, report intentions, request taxi*).

The implementation, in 2008, of obligatory testing, and consequential learning, of plain language proficiency for both pilots and ATCOs switched the focus to non-routine or unexpected events where phraseology alone is not sufficient for communication. In such events, communication is effected by the use of phraseology plus a combination of specific purpose plain language, supported by utterances of "non-domain specific *plain general-purpose* language" (Bullock, 2015, p. 5).

Learning such specific purpose language should be facilitated by teachers who understand the environment in which the communication is taking place (Sarmento, 2011), and have a clear understanding of the context (Douglas, 2000). Classroom materials need to correspond with learning activities to provide a real congruence with students' learning objectives (Paltridge & Starfield, 2013).

Despite ICAO offering global guidance on improving language proficiency in aviation (ICAO, 2010), there has been a tendency to promote plain language alone as the key item of communication. The result is that the onus for language training has been placed on language teachers, many of whom may well find such operational language difficult to comprehend. Teachers, however, must do more than simply get learners to absorb subject focussed material (Richards &

Rodgers, 2001). They should offer learners language from their highly complex and technical domain (Uplinger, 1997), and offer training strategies for real-world communication (Kim & Elder, 2009).

Bullock (2015) proposed re-focussing teaching towards a more appropriate and valid methodology for English learners in the aeronautical domain. He argued that by adopting a more inclusive communicative approach, students' real-world needs would be addressed creating an appropriate and valid learning process.

The methodology suggested an application of three of Brown's (2002) twelve principles for classroom practice, which are particularly important for ESP teaching:

- Principle 2: meaningful learning;

- Principle 4: intrinsic motivation;

- Principle 12: communicative competence.

Meaningful learning implies learning centred on content with relevant to the real-world communication context (Paltridge & Starfield, 2013).

Intrinsic motivation, coming from the actual learner, should be high, due to the amount of personal and professional investment. This can be supported by classroom activities that develop 'survival' and 'repair' strategies (Harmer, 2007, p. 344), such as "paraphrasing and restructuring" (Douglas, 2014, p. 4).

Communicative competence can be enhanced by interactive tasks that have "meaning-focussed input" (Paramasivam, 2013, p. 105) based on specific aeronautical themes and situations.

Bullock (2017) further proposed a conceptual framework supported by a learning-based continuum from which the key focus shifts from testing to learning of real-world communication (see Figure 1). In order therefore to assess how such a methodology could fit into the framework, an initial pilot study was carried out to help provide a platform for further in-depth research. Such research could then deliver a base for developing ESP teacher education.

Participants in the research were 33 student ATCOs, undergoing their basic operational and technical training at the ROMATSA training centre in Constanta, Romania. During this training, students followed two one-week intensive English language classes (three hours per day in two groups) between December 2017 and January 2018. This training aimed to consolidate and improve students' English skills in all six aspects of plain language proficiency (as determined by ICAO, 2010). Participants were aged from 21-32 years old and all had an approximate general English speaking level between Common European Framework of Reference for languages (CEFR) B2 and C1. The group was chosen because the students were being exposed to the proposed methodology and the status of the students as subject matter experts, if only partially due to their trainee status, afforded a key element in the validity of the material and course content.

Figure 1. A learning-based continuum for LSP

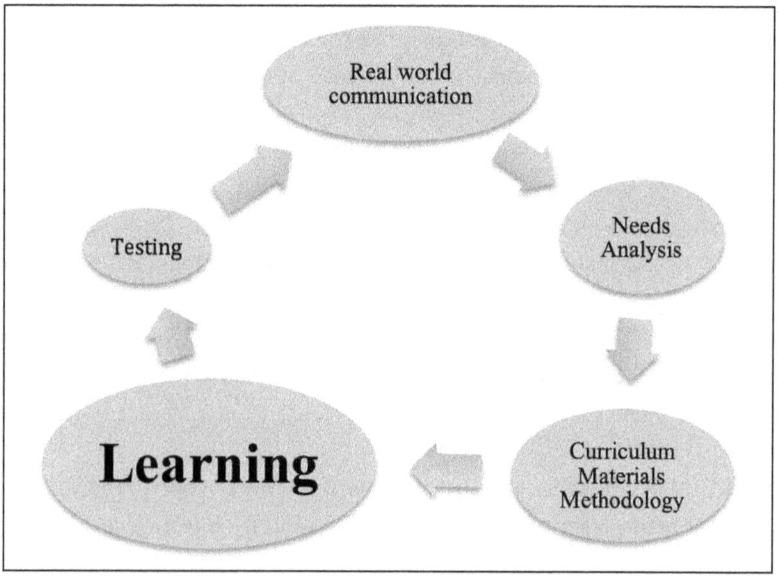

In order to see whether the proposed framework could be adapted to language learning in aeronautical communication, the main research question sought to validate the framework through the methodology and materials as used in the classroom as well as the students' learning objectives. Additionally, in supporting how such a methodology could effectively be implemented in the classroom, it was also important to see how much importance learners placed on the teacher having knowledge and experience of real-world communication. The following section of this paper details the methodology used together with the rationale.

2. Method

2.1. Research methodology

The research was based on a deductive mixed-methods approach, using a concurrent embedded design model (Cresswell, 2009, p. 210). This meant a simultaneous collection of both quantitative (statistical) and qualitative (informational) data, which could be sourced concurrently but evaluated independently. In order to help validate final analyses and conclusions, there was also a need to explore and explain the students' responses, and so sourced data needed to be both measurable (quantitative) and supportive (qualitative). The next section will look at the collection tools and how they were used.

2.2. Data collection

Data were collected from the results of an online survey using *Survey Monkey* completed by the students anonymously and in their own time. All responses were completed between the first and ninth of February 2018, and all students completed the survey, giving a response rate of 100%. Data collection then followed before the results were analysed.

There was a minor concern over the internal validity as the students were able to discuss the course amongst themselves which may have influenced the results.

However, as all students were likely to be motivated and attending classes for their own professional development, these were seen to have a greater influence on the responses. Students were, however, still instructed to complete the survey alone and without reference to colleagues' responses.

Participants (Coded P*n*) were asked to respond to 18 principal statements (coded in the data collection as S*n*) related to the course content and methodology and six post-course sub-statements (coded in the data collection as U*n*) related to how each respondent perceived their increased awareness and knowledge of the language and subject matter[2]. Each statement included a five part Likert scale response (completely agree, agree, neither agree nor disagree, disagree, and completely disagree). The statements were specifically written and the type of response specifically chosen to allow collection of primary quantitative data which could demonstrate a degree of positive or negative correlation between the methodology and the students' expectations in their training objectives. This primary data was to be demonstrated as a positivity coefficient (100%=1.00) relating to the percentage of responses showing completely agree and agree. The rationale was that the higher the coefficient, the more positive the learners see a correlation between the course and their objectives, and thus the more valid the alignment could be with the ESP learning continuum. This method of data collection was chosen as efficient and practical, as it had previously been validated as a way of sourcing similar evidence from a test design project (National Aviation Authority, 2013, 2014).

Secondary qualitative data were obtained from two sources. Firstly, a free response comments option after each of the 18 principal statements in the survey. These were Coded S*n.nn*, corresponding to the statement (S), number (*n*), and free response comment in sequence (.*nn*), according to the order of student participation. Secondly, three free response comment options were presented at the end of all the six U-coded statements. The statements were

---

2. Ten of the main statements related to the overall environment of the course and the requirements of the students' sponsors. Whilst positively responded to, the data was not directly aimed to answer the question for which this research was carried out and so have not been included.

coded FR1-3, and the responses coded FR*n.nn* corresponding to the statement number (FR*n*) and the free response comment in sequence (*.nn*), according to the order of participation.

After completion of the survey, data were obtained and analysed. Firstly, the primary quantitative data were extracted by downloading the survey results as an Excel file that allowed simple numerical data to be calculated with which to assess positivity levels of the various statements. As a more complex data processing tool, such as SPSS, was not available during this pilot study, the data were simplified and shown within the relative limitations of the Excel software. The second stage of data collection investigated comments in the qualitative secondary data which could then be analysed for content and cross-referenced with the intended themes of the study. The data were transferred from the Excel file to a Word document and coded to facilitate referencing. The next section will detail and analyse the results from the study.

3. Results and discussion

3.1. Quantitative data

In line with the research model, the quantitative data were extracted first. The S-coded statements are shown in Table 1 sequentially. Those statements relative to in-course methodologies and materials show extremely positive responses (average coefficient for all, 0.99). Table 1 shows the positivity coefficients with the number of responses under each coefficient.

Responses to the statements relating to post-course students' perceptions on their learning objectives (Table 2) still showed high levels of positivity (average 0.92), although lower than the course content and methodology itself. One student gave a negative response for all six statements relating to post-course perceptions, although the fact that the same student had stated "the course was dynamic and engaging" may indicate simply an error when completing part two of the survey.

Chapter 5

Table 1. Positivity towards in-course methodologies and materials

Code	Statement – in-course methodologies and materials	Pos. n	Neutral	Neg.
S10	The trainer demonstrated a good understanding of how language is used in aeronautical communications.	1.00 33	0.00	0.00
S11	Course activities were varied, interactive, and allowed students to practise using the language learned.	1.00 33	0.00	0.00
S12	The content and context of material during the course was relevant for my training and future work as an ATCO.	1.00 33	0.00	0.00
S13	The lessons included interactive speaking and listening activities.	1.00 33	0.00	0.00
S14	Activities and material included a variety of different aeronautical situations.	0.97 32	0.03 1	0.00
S15	Activities and material focussed on routine and non-routine situations for ATCOs and pilots.	0.94 31	0.06 2	0.00
S17	The material helped improve my vocabulary and structure in an aeronautical communications context.	1.00 33	0.00	0.00
S18	I found the material professionally prepared and presented.	1.00 33	0.00	0.00
	Average	0.99 32.6	0.01 0.4	0.00

Table 2. Positivity of students' post-course perceptions on training objectives

Code	Post-course reaction and opinion	Pos. n	Neutral n	Neg. n
U1	I feel more comfortable about my English skills related to the job of an ATCO.	0.94 31	0.03 1	0.03 1
U2	I am more aware of the difference between plain English and standard phraseologies.	0.94 31	0.03 1	0.03 1
U3	I am more aware of the need for language skills training as part of pilot/ATCO communication.	0.97 32	0 0	0.03 1
U4	I am more aware of the specific language skills required for good language proficiency in pilot/ATCO communications.	0.97 32	0 0	0.03 1
U5	I will use the material from this course as a reference to help maintain my English level.	0.81 27	0.13 4	0.06 2

U6	This type of course is really important for ATCO training.	0.88	0.09	0.03
		29	3	1
	Average	0.92	0.04	0.04
		30.2	1.4	1.4

3.2. Qualitative data

Before making any analytical observations of the qualitative data for trends and correlation with the quantitative findings, the numbers of responses and participation rate are noted for both the principal statements (Table 3) and the second set of statements (Table 4).

Table 3. Final free response comments towards course methodologies and materials

Code	Statement – in-course methodologies and materials	No of comments	Response rate
S10	The trainer demonstrated a good understanding of how language is used in aeronautical communications.	5	15.15%
S11	Course activities were varied, interactive, and allowed students to practise using the language learned.	2	6.06%
S12	The content and context of material during the course was relevant for my training and future work as an ATCO.	4	12.12%
S13	The lessons included interactive speaking and listening activities.	0	-
S14	Activities and material included a variety of different aeronautical situations.	1	3.03%
S15	Activities and material focussed on routine and non-routine situations for ATCOs and pilots.	0	-
S17	The material helped improve my vocabulary and structure in an aeronautical communications context.	0	-
S18	I found the material professionally prepared and presented.	2	6.06%
	Total	14	-
	Average	1.75	5.30%

As Table 3 shows, there were relatively few comments (14) relating to the main statements (response rate 5.3%). In response to the second set of statements,

Table 4 shows participation in the three options (FR1-3), noticeably higher with a total of 68 comments (response rate of 68.69%). The first two statements referring to what students liked most about the course, and what could be done to improve it, showed the highest response rates at 85% and 79% respectively.

Qualitative data thus provided four data sets of informational text from the free response comments in the study – one from responses S10-S18 and three from FR1 to 3. This provided a total of 82 responses. From these data, specific content was identified which could support the theoretical framework, and this is shown in Table 5 (themes coded A to D). Specific qualitative evidence from the statements is given below the table.

Table 4. Free response comments on post-course perceptions and training objectives

Code	Post-course reactions and perceptions – free response	Responses	Response rate
FR1	What did you like most about your aviation English course?	28	84.85%
FR2	This English course could be improved by …	26	78.79%
FR3	Additional Comments	14	42.42%
	Total	68	-
	Average	22	68.69%

Table 5. References to key themes in free response comments

	Research question focus	No of responses	% of total free responses
A	Adaptation of the theoretical framework to language learning for aeronautical communication in the classroom.	41	60.29%
B	Demonstration of congruence between methodology and materials and the learning objectives of students.	35	51.47%
C	Importance placed on the correlation between the teacher having knowledge and experience of real-world communication to enhance such methodology and materials in class.	11	16.18%
D	Learners' perceptions on relevance of methodology and materials to communication in real-life operational situations.	22	32.35%

A clear majority (60%) made reference to how the theoretical framework could be adapted to the language proficiency skills required for aeronautical communication. One student (P20) noted that "we received a lot of information that we can use for our future training", whilst P08 noted that "the material did indeed include a variety of different aeronautical situations". P03 remarked that "I got the chance to speak and practise my aviation English", whilst P11 commented that "it made me more aware of the importance of language proficiency in ATCO communications". Eighteen of the comments referred positively to the need for developing interactive skills for aeronautical communication, twelve of which related to what the students enjoyed most during their course.

In terms of how the methodology and materials achieved congruence with the learning objectives, over half of the respondents commented positively on this. Student P02 stated that the teacher "did his best to teach us plain language for aviation purposes", P04 noted that the teacher "knew what was important for our knowledge", and P05 observed that the teacher knew "exactly what to say and teach us".

The importance placed on the teacher having knowledge and experience of real-world communication to enhance such a methodology in class was less directly commented on (16%). P04 noted that having worked in ATC, the teacher "knew what was important for our knowledge", and P24 stated that the teacher "also shared a lot of his [ATC] experience". P05 also suggested that "it is obvious that the teacher [had worked in ATC] as he knew exactly what to say and teach us".

Finally, the relevance of the course to real-life communications was commented on by 32% of the respondents. In addition to some of the comments noted above, P11 stated that the course "made me more aware of the importance of language proficiency in ATCO communications", P24 additionally observed that "talking about real-life ATCO/pilot radio transmissions [...] can be a good starting point in discussing standard/non-standard issues".

Two additional issues raised are worthy of comment here. The first was that many of the students were apprehensive of their forthcoming exam. Ten comments referred directly to a wish to see more exam preparation through: "more practice" (P03), "emphasis[ing] the requirements" (P06), "more preparation" (P20), and "more exercises and lessons" (P27, P28, P29). The second recurrent theme was the wish to have more learning time for English in aeronautical communications. The word *more* was identified 25 times in the comments relating to the perceived short time given for their training and specific subjects, with many different collocations alluding to the same comment: "I would like *more* hours for practising", noted student P21, "I only wished there was *more* time dedicated" (P08), "Even *more* interactive activities" (P01), having the lessons "*more* often" (P02), "Learning *more* phraseology" (P06, P10, P18, P20, P21, P31, P32), and "*more* listening and speaking" (P24).

4. Discussion

The data analysis showed generally positive responses from the students correlating to the key areas of the research question. Quantitative data was almost unanimously in agreement with the given statements. Qualitative data, whilst less decisive, still showed a very clear majority in favour of how the methodology and materials correlated with the intended rationale of the proposed framework. Students' reactions to the methodology and materials, and the importance of an ESP teacher understanding the real-world target language, was also encouraging and correlated with how well the students perceived meeting their objectives.

The two emerging themes of more exam preparation and additional training, whilst seemingly negative, may actually indicate further support for the proposed framework. As the framework is based on a *learning* ideology rather than a *test* based system, implementation of a more appropriate framework may well alleviate the concern felt amongst students about taking their forthcoming test as training would focus more on the required skills for their professional roles. Secondly, the clear demand for further training in communicative language and skills may well indicate that employing the methodology and material during the course referred to has actually made students even more aware of the need for the required communicative skills in their future roles. This shows that whilst the theoretical approach is targeting the objectives as planned, the suggested length of training to show tangible learning progress may well need to be revisited and lengthened.

5. Conclusions

This pilot study aimed to research whether an emerging learning-based methodology for teaching ESP in the domain of aeronautical communications could be supported by correlating evidence from classroom practice with the theoretical rationale of the framework.

Data sourced from one group of 33 student ATCOs showed clear evidence to support the ideology that focussing on language and communicative skills from the target language domain, as well as employing language teachers with previous experience of the language and communication being taught, is extremely important. Furthermore, employing appropriate teaching methodologies for the required learning objectives in such a domain must also be an integral part of the learning being undertaken if the students are to acquire and improve their language proficiency skills.

Clearly this is an encouraging start which could lead to a more in-depth research project to further support the proposed theory. It is suggested that research could identify and focus on much more specific language and communication, content, and skills, as well as investigating elements of the methodology, material, and activities more thoroughly. The length and content of curriculum development could also be revisited to provide a more appropriate scaffold to promote and encourage appropriate learning as much as possible. Such research could be undertaken directly through classroom practice, as in this study, but should also feed into teacher training courses, particularly those aimed at ESP teachers so teachers are aware of and are trained to use the methodologies and material being proposed.

Finally, any research should look to extend data collection, including increased use of statistical analysis tools for quantitative data, which would offer clearer and more focussed results. Qualitative data could also be extended through focussed face-to-face interviews with students in order to support this.

Acknowledgements

I would like to thank the students, instructors, and administrative managers of ROMATSA during the delivery of this course and the help and assistance given after the course in sourcing the data.

References

Brown, H. D. (2002). English language teaching in the "post method" era – towards better diagnosis, treatment, and assessment. In J. C. Richards & W. A. Renandya (Eds), *Methodology in language teaching* (pp. 9-18). Cambridge University Press. https://doi.org/10.1017/cbo9780511667190.003

Bullock, N. (2015). Wider considerations in teaching speaking of English in the context of aeronautical communications. *IATEFL ESPSIG Journal, 45*, 4-11.

Bullock, N. (2017). *A re-evaluation of washback for learning and testing language in aeronautical communication*. ICAEA, Conference proceedings, Dubrovnik 2017. http://commons.erau.edu/icaea-workshop/2017/monday/19

Creswell, J. W. (2009). *Research design: qualitative, quantitative, and mixed methods approaches* (3rd ed.). Sage Publications.

Douglas, D. (2000). *Assessing language for specific purposes*. Cambridge University Press.

Douglas, D. (2014). *Nobody seems to speak English here today: enhancing assessment and training in aviation English. Iranian Journal of Language Teaching Research, 2*(2), 1-12.

Harmer, J. (2007). *The practice of English language teaching*. Pearson Longman.

ICAO. (2010). *Doc 9835, manual on the implementation of ICAO language proficiency requirements* (2nd ed.). International Civil Aviation Organisation.

Kim, H., & Elder, C. (2009). Understanding aviation English as a lingua franca: perceptions of Korean aviation personnel. *Australian Review of Applied Linguistics, 32*(3), 23.1-23.17. https://doi.org/10.1075/aral.32.3.03kim

National Aviation Authority. (2013). Piloting trial of new level 4 listening material. *NAA Report*, 6-13.

National Aviation Authority. (2014). Piloting trial of new level 4 listening material. *NAA Report*, 1-14.

Paltridge, B., & Starfield, S. (2013). *The handbook of English for specific purposes*. Wiley-Blackwell.

Paramasivam, S. (2013). Materials development for speaking skills in Aviation English for Malaysian air traffic controllers: theory and practice. *Journal of Teaching English for Specific and Academic Purposes, 1*(2), 97-122.

Richards, J. C., & Rodgers, T. S. (2001). *Approaches and methods in language teaching*. Cambridge University Press.

Sarmento, S. (2011). What makes a good aviation English teacher? *Aviation in Focus, 2*(2), 3-5.

Uplinger, S. (1997). English language training for air traffic controllers must go beyond basic ATC vocabulary. *Flight Safety Foundation: Airport Operations, 23*(5), 1-5.

6. Technology-enhanced curriculum development in the ESP tertiary context

Christina Nicole Giannikas[1]

Abstract

Teaching English for Specific Purposes (ESP) in Higher Education (HE) has a long-standing tradition in the language centres of the Cypriot academic world, much like in other European contexts. Even though Cypriot universities are advancing in educational technology, students enter bearing coursebook-led and teacher-centred learning experiences offered in secondary education. The present chapter focusses on a pilot study involving 20 ESP first year students of the Department of Chemical Engineering, and a curriculum that was developed to tailor their academic and professional needs with the aid of a technology-enhanced environment. The aim of the personalised curriculum was to stress the fusion of interactive tools and make use of applications that would deliver opportunities for: (1) autonomy, (2) resource and content management, and (3) communal and individual content production, presentation, and sharing. The impact of the design of the curriculum was investigated through (1) online surveys completed by the students and (2) students' reflection journals. Data reports on the transformational period, the progress made, and the impact the technology-enhanced curriculum had on their learning. Additionally, the investigation revealed insights on the level of intensity of cognitive and instrumental interactivity.

Keywords: technology-enhanced curriculum, pilot study, interactivity, autonomy, transformational learning period.

---

1. Cyprus University of Technology, Limassol, Cyprus; christina.giannikas@cut.ac.cy; https://orcid.org/0000-0002-5653-6803

How to cite this chapter: Giannikas, C. N. (2019). Technology-enhanced curriculum development in the ESP tertiary context. In S. Papadima-Sophocleous, E. Kakoulli Constantinou & C. N. Giannikas (Eds), *ESP teaching and teacher education: current theories and practices* (pp. 95-110). Research-publishing.net. https://doi.org/10.14705/rpnet.2019.33.928

Chapter 6

1. Introduction

Teaching ESP in HE has a long-standing tradition in academic contexts where language instructors are expected to adjust their curriculum to the needs of students of various departments and faculties. More specifically, in the Cypriot HE context, language centres operate separately from other departments and focus on teaching English and communicative skills in a specific field. Students, however, enter university bearing coursebook-led and teacher-centred learning experiences (Tsagari & Giannikas, 2018), having not used their familiarity of technology for educational purposes in secondary education (Papadima-Sophocleous, Kakoulli-Constantinou, & Giannikas, 2014). This creates barriers for university students, and challenges for language instructors.

The present pilot study focusses on 20 ESP first year students of the Department of Chemical Engineering, and a curriculum that was developed to tailor their academic and professional needs with the aid of a technology-enhanced environment. The students were encouraged to use electronic means instead of paper. The aim of the specific personalised curriculum was to stress the fusion of the interactive tools provided from a constructivist or socio-constructivist approach, a scientific position that knowledge arises via interaction and active construction (Mascolo & Fischer, 2005), and makes use of applications that would deliver opportunities for:

- autonomy;

- resource and content management; and

- communal and individual content production, presentation, and sharing (Hall & Conboy, 2009).

The data of the present pilot study reports on the students' transformational period, the progress they made and the students' perception of the impact the specific technology-enhanced curriculum had on their language learning and attitude towards the process. Additionally, the investigation revealed insights on the level of intensity of cognitive (between participants) and instrumental (between participants and technology) interactivity. Through the outcomes of the study, the researcher aspires to share a complete curriculum overview, present how technology-enhanced environments can pedagogically benefit ESP courses, and prompt the re-evaluation of curriculum design and delivery in HE ESP by embracing students' academic needs.

1.1. A background review

There is a growing global demand for the teaching of ESP, and the purpose of its courses is to provide students with in-context language and authentic tasks that are related to the learners' professional needs. Ideally, students would be motivated to develop competencies necessary to develop the L2 and achieve their language learning goals (Živković, 2016). What distinguishes ESP and keeps it in demand is its approach and decisions related to content and teaching methods are based on the students' motives for learning the foreign language (Dudley-Evans & St John, 1998). For this reason, there is a call for highly specific ESP courses to be implemented in the experimental needs-based syllabus as part of a renewal process (Richards, 2001). Needs can involve what learners know, do not know, or want to know, and can be collected and analysed in a number of ways (Hyland, 2006). The integration of technology can help assist these needs (Higgins & Spitulnik, 2008).

Integrating technology in the ESP learning environment provides potential for an innovative teaching and learning approach based on elements of communication, interaction, and cooperation, which relates to earlier Vygotskian (1962) research on cognitive development and social learning. Therefore, expecting ESP learners to develop into successful, autonomous students is not feasible in a traditional teacher-centred classroom where the instructor dominates the learning process (Hedge, 2000). Hedge's (2000) observation supports Lekatompessy's (2010) statement that in order to improve learning, the students' needs must be considered. In other words, the development of an effective curriculum should include as much information as possible about the needs of the learners. Skehan (1998) goes as far as arguing that using coursebooks is against all notions of learnercentredness. ESP students require materials and learning scenarios outside the limitations of traditional teaching (Gimeno-Sanz, 2014). More specifically, the ongoing development of ESP and curriculum design have verified Bojovic's (2006) conclusion that resources should be authentic, up-to-date, and relevant for the students' specialisations. Integrating a technology-enhanced ESP curriculum can provide university students with a variety of learning opportunities and advantages ranging from interactive and communicative activities related to their field of interest, to tools for giving feedback and self-awareness (Butler-Pascoe & Wilburg, 2003). This would mean that developing a successful curriculum prioritises and looks into the appropriate learning needs and interests of the learner, rather than focussing exclusively on the content they would be learning. For this reason, design practices have also been enhanced by skillful uses of technology. New technologies have offered new ways of visualising and capturing curriculum designs, bringing authenticity and collaboration to what has been a risk-averse process (Giannikas, 2019). Bringing these processes and practices into sharper focus as students look for a wider range of benefits from their courses can be an ongoing challenge. Nonetheless, using technology to enhance an ESP curriculum can assist universities, and those studying or working with them, to gain an advantage. However, the time sensitive nature of most ESP HE courses, needs analysis, and curriculum development have limited investigations of processes and contexts of technology-enhanced ESP curriculum design. The present chapter aims to contribute to the literature by disseminating the outcomes of the pilot study.

1.2. The curriculum

The present ESP curriculum consisted of two dimensions: (1) L2 delivery and (2) employment awareness. Therefore, the design of the curriculum aimed to enhance the students' ability required in order to successfully communicate in the L2 within their occupational and academic context. The module was not supported by any coursebooks, due to the limited material for this specific science in ESP and because students' needs were taken into consideration. All material used was prepared by the instructor and the course outline was communicated and shared with the students before the semester commenced. To equip the students with appropriate and tailor-made material, the instructor took the students' L1 and L2 background into consideration, as well as the content they would come across in their other modules. The following list displays the main areas of the curriculum:

- academic journals (analysis and comprehension);
- academic writing;
- communication skills expected in academic contexts;
- presentations and responding to questions;
- lab communication; and
- research skills (conducted online)

The fusion of interactive tools was supported by Social Media, Google Scholar, Google Drive/Docs/Forms/Slides, YouTube, Canvas, and Prezi. This 13-week course took place in a Multimedia Language Classroom (MLC) for three hours a week, and all students had access to an individual computer. The MLC had a projector, and students were also encouraged to use their mobile phones for a number of tasks. Paper was not used at all during the semester and students worked on their activities or assignments exclusively on online tools. The use of the online interactive tools are displayed in Table 1.

Table 1. The application of online interactive tools

Interactive Tools	Use Of Tools
Social Media	As a Course Management System (CMC), discussion platform, for the submission of activities
Google Scholar	Online search for academic journals
Google Drive	Management and organisation of material, sharing of folders, reflection keeping
Google Docs	Collaborate on assignments, articles, projects, instant sharing with instructor and peers, journal paper break down, review and analysis, reflection writing
Google Forms	Creation of questionnaires for research projects
Google Slides	Presentations and the use of single slides for covers/ posters, presentations for mock conference participations
YouTube	Listening tasks, vocabulary/terminology activities, note-taking tasks, sharing clips to exchange information, creation of a clip playlist for conference presentation inspiration
Canvas	Creation of lab posters, safety posters, professional bio posters
Press	Interactive presentations between students and instructor

2. Method

2.1. Data collection

The current pilot study was conducted in order to trial a new ESP curriculum. The research, as mentioned earlier, focussed on 20 first year undergraduate students and the effect their ESP curriculum had on their autonomy, resource/content management, and communal and individual content production, presentation, and sharing. For the needs of the pilot study, data was gathered through students' reflective journals and questionnaires.

The students were encouraged to create folders on Google Drive and save all their reflections in the folders. They were not requested to answer specific questions. The students were expected to complete their reflection entries weekly and share their thoughts regarding the development of the course, their language learning, and how they progressed through the semester. These thoughts were only shared with their instructor. The reason the students were given this freedom was to (1) include their needs and thoughts in any potential changes made to the curriculum, (2) encourage them to share their opinions and input freely, and (3) identify what the students found most useful and intriguing during their lessons. This approach was applied in order to avoid guided and biased reflections.

The data that derived from the reflections were analysed and coded on Atlas.ti 7^2 (Scientific Software Development GmbH, Berlin), and themes emerged as a result of the coding on the software. The questionnaires, which were distributed at the end of the semester, aimed to provide insights on students' thoughts about technology-enhanced learning and their demographic information. The questionnaires were created on Google Forms and included multiple choice and open-ended questions. The questionnaires were analysed on the response spreadsheet.

---

2. https://atlasti.com/2012/08/15/atlas-ti-7-qualitative-data-analysis-software-gets-work-done-efficiently-smoothly-enjoyably/

2.2. The context and the participants

The English language courses at Cyprus University of Technology (CUT) are mandatory for students of all university faculties, i.e. English for Geotechnical Sciences and Environmental Management, English for Management and Economics, English for Applied Arts and Communication, English for Health Sciences (Athanasiou et al., 2016) and, since September 2017, English for Chemical Engineering.

All ESP courses take place in MLCs, where students have access to an individual computer. All students and instructors have access to Moodle, which is CUT's CMC.

Based on the demographic data, 15 of the students were female and five were male. The students were all Cypriot and shared the same native language (Standard Modern Greek) and dialect (Greek Cypriot Dialect). The male students were 20 years of age and their female peers were 18. This is due to the fact that Cypriot male students must complete their two-year military service immediately after they graduate from secondary school. Furthermore, 56.9% of the students had been learning English for nine to 12 years and 43.1% for six to eight years.

According to the questionnaire responses, 64.3% of the students did not use technology in their language lessons at school, however, 50% of the students sometimes used technology in their general education in secondary school. A high percentage, 92.9%, of the students stated that the majority of their English lessons were based on coursebooks. Nonetheless, 57.1% stated that they would have preferred that their language lessons at school included the use of technology. Some indicative responses are as follows:

> "Technology can be more vivid and interesting, but it is trickier to use" (Student 4).

> "You can access more information" (Student 1).

> "I prefer technology because it is easy to use, and you can find more things which can help you in your subjects" (Student 11).

> "I cannot concentrate on a screen for long" (Student 19).

> "Books can be really interesting sometimes, but working on the internet can be fun and entertaining" (Student 15).

3. Results and discussion

3.1. Questionnaire outcomes

The ESP curriculum was based on activities and projects that could be carried out on a computer, which was the main equipment used for the needs of the course. According to the outcomes of the questionnaire, the curriculum embraced and encouraged autonomy in language learning, as stated by all the participants. More specifically, students believed that certain activities seemed more appealing as seen in the following sample statements:

> "I enjoy using technology in my English classes because I use critical thinking rather than just accepting everything I see or hear" (Student 2).

> "I can use the internet and answer my own questions. I don't need to ask my professor for answers all the time" (Student 7).

> "This kind of learning and using technology in my lessons helps me become more mature as a student" (Student 20).

The majority of the students (64.3%) understood their progress and became more independent from one semester to the next. The questionnaire, used for the needs of the study, focussed on the main tools applied to deliver content, and prompted the respondents' impression of them.

3.1.1. Facebook Group: English for Chemical Engineering

The Facebook closed group was used throughout the course for students to post their activities, get involved in class discussions, and stay informed concerning class/university announcements their instructor posted. According to the data, none of the students had experience in using any kind of social media for educational purposes, and 71.4% of the respondents stated that it was very practical and preferred sharing/posting their work with their instructor and peers via Facebook, rather than handing in a hard copy of their assignment or uploading it on Moodle. They also found Facebook convenient because they received notifications on their mobile phones whenever there was activity on the Facebook group. It is important to add that none of the students had anything negative to state regarding the use of Facebook for the needs of their ESP course.

The use of social media can be controversial in a number of learning contexts. In this case, students were not aware of how they could use Facebook in a pedagogical way, which meant there was a form of 'training' in the fall semester. Students were given time limits on Facebook (i.e. a task would need to be completed in 10, 15 minutes, etc.), and were expected to post their work in a timely manner. Their post was deleted if there was any form of plagiarism (which was detected via Turnitin) and students were asked to re-work the task so that it met codes of academic integrity. This is an interesting shift for students who have spent their entire schooling working in a teacher-centred, coursebook-led learning environment.

3.1.2. YouTube

According to findings, the participating students had never used YouTube for pedagogical purposes in the past, and it was the tool that brought about the most positive responses, with only one respondent stating that they believed it to be distracting. Over half of the respondents (57.1%) stated that they enjoyed using YouTube due to the fact that their listening tasks had a visual, and 71.4% enjoyed using subtitles, which worked as a safety-net during some of the more challenging activities, and gave the students the incentive of becoming more autonomous. For example, students were asked not to use subtitles throughout the clips, but were encouraged to use them when they had difficulty making sense of what they were watching. The subtitles used were in English, which helped students with their phonological as well as lexical understanding. A smaller percentage (21.4%) of the students stated that they enjoyed using YouTube because there was more variety in the activities, and there was fruitful information regarding the topic at hand. During the course, students viewed TED Talks, university lectures, conference presentations, and lab guidelines in the field of chemical engineering in the L2. According to the multiple choice questions of the questionnaire, 100% of the students believed that their exposure to the YouTube tasks helped them in their other modules as well as in ESP, and prompted them to use YouTube as a resource for the rest of their studies. With the specific YouTube activities students were presented with, they were encouraged to develop their note-taking skills and enhance the ability to analyse and focus on important points of what they heard and saw in the clips. Finally, YouTube was used as a virtual library to support the ESP content by providing students with access to videos, allowing them to better illustrate complex concepts, procedures, and ideas.

3.1.3. Google Docs/Drive

The findings have shown that none of the students were familiar, or had even heard of, Google Docs and Google Drive before. The initial reason the students were introduced to the two tools was to help them organise their work on the Drive, go back when they needed to study, and reflect on their learning by creating a 'My Reflections' folder. Google Docs was used exclusively throughout the semester, due to the instructor's 'no paper' policy. This approach is aligned with Green Office Practices, designed to save paper and meet several environmental objectives in HE (Zen et al., 2016). The students were familiar with the concept of sustainable development and waste deduction given that they studied solid waste management. Students were encouraged to 'go green' during their ESP classes as well, which was communicated to them from the beginning of the semester, to which no one brought any objections. More specifically, 100% of the respondents found the sharing feature very useful and practical, and 64.3% of the students appreciated the fact that they did not need to save their work constantly. A smaller percentage, 28.6% stated that it was easier to use than Microsoft Word. After becoming more familiar with Google Drive and Google Docs, none of the students wanted to use Moodle to upload their assignments any more.

3.1.4. Google Slides and PowerPoint

Students were encouraged to use the information they received from YouTube university lectures and conference abstracts found online, to prepare presentations on various topics in the field of chemical engineering. They were given the option to use Google Slides or PowerPoint. The vast majority (82%) of the participants preferred using Google Slides. All students stated that they enjoyed the creative element of preparing their slides and finding information and data to display. Nonetheless, the majority of the students had negative feelings towards presentations. Half of the students did not feel comfortable using English to deliver presentations in front of their peers, and 14.1% stated that the entire process made them very nervous. A small percentage (28.6%) enjoyed giving presentations and stated they learned from the process. None of the students had ever given a presentation before, and they had not been assigned such tasks in their other modules either. Although this is a basic skill and task in HE, the students in Cypriot universities bear very little experience presenting in their native language, which justifies that half of the students felt uneasy presenting in a foreign language.

The combination of the use of various tools and the very different learning environment helped students develop various skills and become more autonomous. According to the questionnaire data, 64.3% stated they asked their instructor less questions in the second semester than in the first, and all the participants felt they had a better understanding of the course. From the responses gathered, one could interpret that students enjoyed working together, collaborating, and interacting via technology. A percentage of 64.3% stated they found working on group projects effective (e.g. preparing a group presentation, analysing an academic paper, or comparing notes of a lecture viewed on YouTube). Based on the data, none of the students wanted to work alone on coursebooks after following a curriculum that embraced technology and collaborative learning and eliminated paper and teacher-centred coursebook-led approaches. The present ESP experience prompted 72% of the students to state that they were more confident English users than they ever were in their past schooling. This was mostly due to the fact that students felt they were exposed to more authentic and realistic language and situations. They were using tools that they would apply in their everyday life and work with material adjusted to their academic and linguistic needs.

3.2. Students' reflections

As mentioned in the Methods section, the students participating in the study kept a reflective journal in Google Drive, which they only shared with the instructor. Here they were encouraged to reflect on the course weekly, explaining how they saw themselves develop as university students. The reflections helped the instructor understand students' needs, and how the curriculum affected their learning. It also gave students a better understanding of their own foreign language development, and gave them the incentive to look at the process of language learning critically.

The reflections' outcomes added value to the course of the study as they offered students a voice. Furthermore, the students' insights added to the outcomes of the questionnaire. The two approaches of data collection strengthened, validated, and complemented each other due to the fact that the reflections provided a better understanding and explanation of the figures that derived from the analysis of the questionnaires. The reflections were coded for analysis and, as a result, the following themes emerged:

- intrigued by technology;
- increased confidence;
- autonomy;
- student interaction;
- rich resources; and
- learned more about their field via the ESP course.

Here, a sample and interpretations of final reflections of the course are displayed below:

"Looking back at the beginning of the first semester, and the beginning of the ESP lessons, I have concluded that it was going to be an **awesome course** throughout the whole semester **due to the expansion of the usage of technology** during classes. Now that we are nearly at the end of the second semester I **feel more confident** about myself speaking English in front of other people. Moreover, using technology helped me to emphasise more on researching the web and finding the answers for questions that nobody could give me answers to. Also, I've also learned **how to cooperate** with other people in the making of a project or a presentation. I found this very interesting because during the preparation we all shared our thoughts about a specific subject and exchanged different ideas. In conclusion, this second semester of English taught me how to be more independent and more competitive in my life" (Student 15).

"During the second semester, we have learned a lot of things in our English course that helped us, not only with our studies, but also with other courses. **We watched videos, lectures from chemical engineers talking about their experiments, the solution of their experiments and their plans for the future about chemical engineering.** We had so **many resources** because we were working online. I learned more than I had ever expected from an English class. It was all very helpful" (Student 4).

"In the lesson of English during the second semester, we learned many new things. To begin with, the lesson was more specific and had to do with chemical engineering, not with academic skills in general. Therefore, we enhanced our knowledge with issues connected to chemical engineering, and even how **to approach a scientific paper correctly**. In addition, we used YouTube for listening, PowerPoint, Canvas (to create posters) and other useful technological tools that made the lesson **more appealing.** Furthermore, we **interacted** with

Chapter 6

> our fellow students and **collaborated** through presentations and this is something that **we are going to need later on in life,** not to mention that we got an idea of how a lecture is but in an easier way, as we were able to put subtitles and stop it, or go back and hear something again. Overall, in my opinion the course was easier to understand and closer to the subject of our studies because of the material we used" (Student 18).

When combining questionnaire figures and reoccurring reflection statements, results show that the majority of the students viewed the technology-enhanced curriculum as a positive feature of the course. In reflections, students mentioned the use of YouTube and presentations extensively, as these had an impact and would help students develop skills they would need in their academic and professional path. The analysis of student responses suggests that students valued and profited from the opportunity to take up a more autonomous, student-centred, constructivist approach to learning. Their reflections indicate that they perceived improvement in their ability to work with each other, work online, and increase their knowledge of English for Chemical Engineering.

4. Conclusions

The study discussed in this chapter offers a comprehensive up-to-date overview of the findings generated from a pilot study of technology-enhanced curriculum development in ESP. Research findings indicate the transformational process and development of the participants as digital learners and users. The present study, however, is not without limitations. Although this was a pilot study, the sample size was considerably small. A larger sample size would ensure a representative distribution of the population of ESP students. Furthermore, the study would have benefitted from an additional semester of data collection, and although this was not possible in the current context, it can be tackled in other future research projects.

The findings in this line of inquiry elicited some enriched and complementary findings which revealed insights on the level of intensity of cognitive and instrumental interactivity. This leads to an important outcome of the study, which was that a coursebook, teacher-centred context can be overcome with ease when students are encouraged to apply mechanisms and tools they are accustomed to and use in their own daily lives. A technology-enhanced curriculum can encourage students to develop as autonomous learners and embrace a wider variety of content and resources in a student-centred environment. The pilot study has provided a humble attempt to show that the Cypriot, and similar contexts, are ready to leave their traditional coursebook-heavy approaches behind, and embrace a constructivist approach in a digitally rich ESP curriculum.

Acknowledgements

I would like to thank the Chemical Engineer students of CUT for their cooperation and insights. Their input has proven very valuable.

References

Athanasiou, A., Constantinou, E., Neophytou, M., Nicolaou, A., Papadima-Sophocleous, S., & Yerou, C. (2016). Aligning ESP courses with the Common European Framework of Reference for Languages. *Language Learning in Higher Education, 6*(2), 297-316 https://doi.org/10.1515/cercles-2016-0015

Bojovic, M. (2006). Teaching foreign languages for specific purposes: teacher development. *The proceedings of the 31st Annual Association of Teacher Education in Europe* (pp. 487-493). Portorož - Ljubljana.

Butler-Pascoe, M. E., & Wilburg, K. M. (2003). Technology and teaching English language learners. Pearson Education Inc.

Dudley-Evans, T., & St John, M. J. (1998). Developments in English for specific purposes: a multidisciplinary approach. Cambridge University Press.

Giannikas, C. N. (2019). *Technology-enhanced curriculum development: a focus on the ESP Tertiary Context.* TESOL Convention, Atlanta, USA.

Gimeno-Sanz, A. M. (2014). Fostering learner autonomy in technology-enhanced ESP courses. In E. Barcena, T. Read & J. Arás (Eds), Languages for specific purposes in the digital era. Educational Linguistics (vol 19). Springer. https://doi.org/10.1007/978-3-319-02222-2_2

Hall, R., & Conboy, H. (2009). *Connecting transitions and independent learning in higher education: evaluating the impact of the read/write web on the first-year student experience.* EDULEARN09.

Hedge, T. (2000). Teaching and learning in the language classroom. Oxford University Press.

Higgins, T. E., & Spitulnik, M. W. (2008). Supporting teachers' use of technology in science instruction through professional development: a literature review. *Journal of Science Education and Technology, 17*(5), 511-521. https://doi.org/10.1007/s10956-008-9118-2

Hyland, K. (2006). English for academic purposes: an advanced resource book. Routledge

Lekatompessy, F. M. (2010). *Needs analysis in curriculum development.* https://upipasca.wordpress.com/2010/02/19/needs-analysis-in-curriculum-development/

Mascolo, M. F., & Fischer, K. W. (2005). *Constructivist theories. Cambridge Encyclopedia of Child Development* (pp. 49-63). Cambridge University Press.

Papadima-Sophocleous, S., Kakoulli-Constantinou, E., & Giannikas, C. N. (2014). Teachers' attitudes towards the use of technology in EFL within public junior secondary schools in Cyprus. In M. Dodigovic (Ed.), *Attitudes to technology in ESL/EFL pedagogy.* TESOL Arabia Publications.

Richards, J. C. (2001). Curriculum development in language teaching. Cambridge University Press.

Skehan, P. (1998). *A cognitive approach to language learning.* Oxford University Press.

Tsagari, D., & Giannikas, C. N. (2018). Re-evaluating the use of L1 in the second language classroom: students vs. teachers. *Applied Linguistics Review.* https://doi.org/10.1515/applirev-2017-0104

Vygotsky, L. S. (1962). *Thought and language.* MIT Press.

Zen, I., Subramaniam, D., Sulaiman, H., Saleh, A. L., Omar, W., & Salim, M. (2016). Institutionalize waste minimization governance towards campus sustainability: a case study of Green Office initiatives in Universiti Teknologi Malaysia. *Journal of Cleaner Production, 135,* 1407-1422. https://doi.org/10.1016/j.jclepro.2016.07.053

Živković S (2016). The ESP technology-supported learning environment. *European Journal of Social Sciences Education and Research, 6*(1), 154-162.

7. Embedding a serious game into an ESP curriculum

Giouli Pappa[1] and Salomi Papadima-Sophocleous[2]

Abstract

This paper describes how a selected Commercial Off-The-Shelf (COTS) Serious Game (SG) was evaluated before being integrated into an English for Specific Purposes (ESP) curriculum. Echoing the concerns of language practitioners regarding the adoption of SGs into their teaching practices, this paper describes the steps and decisions taken before the selected COTS SG implementation into a specific learning context; that of the course English for shipping at the Cyprus University of Technology (CUT). A combination of methods was initiated towards assessing the COTS SG. It was carried out following the qualitative embedded single case study research design, as this research explores only one case; that of the assessment of the SG called *Escape From Desolo*. The aim of the case study was to explore the areas of ESP teaching with COTS SGs by illustrating a combination of assessment methods that could be adopted by those considering SG embedding in formal ESP language settings. The present chapter first outlines the reasons which initiated such integration. The initial assessment of the selected SG and the game design, which is carried out with the use of the Relevance, Embedding, Transfer, Adaptation, Immersion, and Naturalisation (RETAIN) model, is discussed. This is followed by further evaluation of the particular SG, which occurred with the use of the four-dimensional framework. After evaluating its pedagogical use, an analysis of the application of the selected tool

---

1. Cyprus University of Technology, Limassol, Cyprus; giouli.pappa@cut.ac.cy; https://orcid.org/0000-0002-8844-0435

2. Cyprus University of Technology, Limassol, Cyprus; salomi.papadima@cut.ac.cy; https://orcid.org/0000-0003-4444-4482

How to cite this chapter: Pappa, G., & Papadima-Sophocleous, S. (2019). Embedding a serious game into an ESP curriculum. In S. Papadima-Sophocleous, E. Kakoulli Constantinou & C. N. Giannikas (Eds), *ESP teaching and teacher education: current theories and practices* (pp. 111-129). Research-publishing.net. https://doi.org/10.14705/rpnet.2019.33.929

within the curriculum is presented. Both the model and the framework are presented in detail in the chapter. Although this study focusses on English for shipping, it is hoped that this process may be applied in different ESP contexts for future studies. The results of the evaluation of the chosen SG with the use of the model and the framework indicated their usefulness in assessing a SG intended to be used in an ESP teaching and learning context. It is hoped that this case can prove beneficial in other ESP learning contexts.

Keywords: formal education, serious games, COTS, Escape From Desolo, RETAIN, four-dimensional framework.

1. Introduction

1.1. Background

Nowadays, there is a noticeably growing tendency to reform the pedagogical approaches within the formal education systems in ways that facilitate the learning processes and cater to the learners' needs (Care, Kim, Vista, & Anderson, 2018). This tendency is vastly associated with rapid technological advancements that occur and therefore, shape the way people work, live, and/or learn (Hutchinson & Waters, 1987). One such technological advancement is that of SGs.

SGs are defined and interpreted from a range of different viewpoints: Zyda (2005) sees them as "a mental contest, played with a computer in accordance with specific rules that uses entertainment to further government or corporate training, education, health, public policy, and strategic communication objectives" (p. 26). More broadly, Michael and Chen (2005) describe SGs as computer-based games that include more purposes than pure entertainment. SGs have a long history in training in army and nursing or even aviation flight contexts (Djaouti, Alvarez, Jessel, & Rampnoux, 2011). Their simulated environment ensures that crew have the experience to safely and efficiently deal with offshore situations and real-life emergency situations such as escaping from buildings and so forth (Djaouti et al., 2011).

This history of SGs in training is still prevalent in the maritime industry as considerable interest has been devoted to the pursuit of learning through, and with them. The cost-effective 'edutainment' nature of SGs offers the potential to facilitate both formal and informal learning (Vintimilla-Tapia et al., 2018, p. 25). As stated by Arnab et al. (2012),

> "[m]any studies point to the positive qualities of SG, such as their persuasiveness and motivational appeal, which can support immersive, situated and learner-centred learning experiences (Aldrich, 2009; David & Watson, 2008 [...]). Proponents of SGs see them as a means for active construction, rather than passive reception of knowledge [(Karshenas & Haber, 2012)], and as prime opportunities to practise key soft skills like problem-solving, decision making, inquiry multitasking, collaboration, and creativity [(Baldauf et al., 2016)]" (p. 159).

1.2. Context

This extensive adoption of SGs in maritime studies for experiencing real-life situations (Baldauf et al., 2016) was also considered in the ESP course of the CUT Language Centre (LC). Synergies between the LC ESP teaching staff and the related CUT specific discipline staff take place annually in order to evaluate, develop, and continuously and systematically improve the ESP curricula. Such curricula are usually competency-based, centred on what students know and can do, characterised by the affluence of technology that shapes the way people work, live, and learn, and they are dictated by the demands of the labour market (of any specific workplace such as the army, nursing, aviation, and maritime, as mentioned earlier) (Robertson, 2019).

Following this process, the integration of an already-made SG was considered for the development of the English for shipping curriculum at the end of the academic year 2017-2018. The *Escape From Desolo* COTS SG was primarily

Chapter 7

selected for its fantasy/story content relevance to the safety at sea curriculum component and its cost free nature. *Escape From Desolo* (Figure 1) was created by the Uniteam Training Oil & Gas, Marine, and Industrial Sector company in 2015. It originally intended to educate/train the prosper seafarers about the safety at sea conventions, shipboard procedures, and onboard emergencies in an engaging way. Through instant feedback loops, badges, progress bars, and leaderboards aligned with learning objectives, it primarily aimed to reduce the ever-shortening attention spans and the frequent dropouts or retention rates observed with more traditional teaching. The goal of the game is for a young cadet (the player) to disembark from 'Desolo', a small container ship, and take shore leave so he can meet up with his beloved girlfriend Eve in Hamburg; yet, he needs to go over some obstacles in his way. The cadet must use his wits and skills to navigate safety hazards, respond to alarms and drills, negotiate with a port state control officer, solve puzzles, work safely, stay healthy, follow shipboard procedures, and make sure the reputation of the owners of the Desolo is preserved. *Escape From Desolo* was the first SG for seafarers designed to improve behavioural based safety onboard ships, and it was originally designed for the training classroom of the company.

Figure 1. Escape From Desolo SG

This research deals with the assessment a COTS SG used in a particular industry, that of maritime industry, which is closely related to the particular ESP in question, that of English for shipping, prior to its integration in the language programme. More specifically, since the particular game has not been developed for ESP classes, the aim is to explore ways of assessing it before its use in an ESP class to find out whether it can actually be suitable for such teaching and learning contexts (English for shipping). If it proves suitable through the assessment processes examined in this chapter, it would add to innovative teaching approaches to ESP learning. Moreover, the SG assessment processes and assessment tools may prove beneficial to practitioners considering assessing a SG before integrating game-based learning and SG in their programmes.

The idea of enriching teaching approaches to the CUT LC ESP curriculum, and more particularly to that of English for shipping, triggered the interest in exploring the use of the COTS SG introduction, and as a result, a first interest in assessing such a case: assessing the selected game and game design regarding its content, and secondly, the way it would be applied within the learning context. These considerations shaped the following research questions.

- How does the assessment of the COTS SG named *Escape From Desolo* through the use of the RETAIN model justify the selection of the particular game for its use in English for shipping?

- How does the dimension of pedagogical considerations of the four-dimensional framework correspond to those of English for shipping?

- Which pedagogic approaches can support learning outcomes and activities?

To answer these questions, the authors initiated a single-case research study prior to the game's classroom implementation to evaluate the *Escape From Desolo* game and game design and pedagogic use for integration into an ESP curriculum.

2. Research method

This study was based on a qualitative embedded single case study design with multiple sub-units of analysis. This type of research design requires a systematic collection of either an individual, a group, or a community. They examine social settings or events for the purpose of gaining insights into their functioning (Yin, 1994, Schreiber & Asner-Self, 2011). In this study, the case of the initial assessment of *Escape From Desolo*, prior to its implementation in an ESP programme, constitutes the main unit of research.

This case study entails only one case of SGs and therefore the research findings are limited to this type of SG and its related ESP context implementation. However, it explores a set of game assessment processes which were followed in order to prepare the implementation of the SG in the particular ESP environment. This combination of methods is yet to be documented in assessing COTS SGs, at least to the researchers' best knowledge. Based on this, the data was collected through heuristic inquiry. Heuristic inquiry is an adaptation of the phenomenological inquiry. It is an experience-based technique (Djuraskovic & Arthur, 2010). It involves problem-solving and self-reflection; the researcher is expected to be involved in the research process in a disciplined manner (Djuraskovic & Arthur, 2010, Kocdar, Okur, & Bozkurt, 2017, p. 54). As such, the researchers participated in the whole procedure by selecting the framework models to be enforced as typical examples of assessing games and their educational value for curriculum development.

The RETAIN model framework – developed by Gunter, Kenny, and Vick (2008) to assess games and game design, was utilised in order to assess how well *Escape From Desolo* contains and incorporates the educational content of safety at sea (Research Question 1). Therefore, the RETAIN's aspects constitute the (first) sub-units of analysis. To inform the way *Escape From Desolo* could be applied within the ESP curriculum (Research Question 2), the researchers further employed the four-dimensional framework of de Freitas and Oliver (2006). This framework was particularly chosen as it is one of the few that provides a tool (a table to focus on specific issues) to help practitioners incorporate games in practice in such a way as to ensure a smooth continuum from theory/planning to deployment and evaluation. As a rather non-prescriptive approach, it is the only one, to the researchers' current knowledge, that allows educational designers to consider a more user-based and specialised set of educationally specific factors (De Freitas & Oliver, 2006) (Research Question 3). Therefore, the four aspects of the framework are considered as (the second) sub-units of analysis.

2.1. The RETAIN model

Escape From Desolo COTS SG was initially selected by the authors regarding its cost free nature and its fantasy/story content relevance to the safety at sea curriculum component. Yet, recent literature notes that the selection of an educational game to be integrated signifies more than its attractive content or fantasy story, or even the fact that "it will eventually teach something" (Ulicsak, 2010, p. 56). It presupposes a strong correlation between the academic content and the relevance, embedding, transfer, adaptation, immersion, and naturalisation aspects of the game (Gunter et al., 2008). The model known as RETAIN, which was developed to assess games and game design in general, is based on three existing theories: (1) Keller's attention, relevance, confidence/challenge, and satisfaction/success model, (2) Gagne's events of instruction, and (3) Piaget's ideas on schema. Each of the RETAIN aspects is further divided into four levels: 0, 1, 2, 3. "Level 3 means that there is a strong correlation between the game and that relevant aspect, while Level 0 indicates the game does not meet that aspect" (Gunter et al., 2008, p. 520).

In his table on page 59, Ulicsak (2010) describes the six aspects that are required for appropriate SGs.

With 'relevance', he refers to the way materials should be presented to learners, and the necessity for the material to be relevant to the learners' needs and learning styles. He also stresses the need of relevance of instructional units with each other so that everything links together and it is built upon previous work.

A second required aspect for appropriate SGs according to Uliscak (2010) is 'embedding'. This refers to the assessment that has to take place to ensure that the academic content is linked with the fantasy/story content (narrative structure, storylines, player, experience, dramatic structure, fictive elements, etc.).

Chapter 7

The third aspect required for appropriate SGs according to Uliscak (2010) is 'transfer'. This refers to the ability of the player to use previous knowledge in other areas.

'Adaptation' is the fourth required aspect for appropriate SGs. This is about the ability of the learners to change their behaviour as a result of the transfer.

'Immersion' refers to the ability of the player to intellectually invest in the context of the game.

Finally, Ulicsak (2010) refers to 'naturalisation' as the fifth aspect required for appropriate SGs. This makes reference to the development of habitual and spontaneous use of information the players gain while playing the game.

Gunter and colleagues, though, have further ordered the aspects based on their importance in a context that involved both game designers and instructors/professors (Gunter et al., 2008). They created a rubric that enables the educators and game designers to assess the importance of the games. "Specifically, they had ordered the aspects from the least to the most important, as follows: Relevance, Immersion, Embedding, Adaption, Transfer and Naturalisation" (Gunter et al., 2008, p. 527). The RETAIN weighting chart is illustrated in Table 1.

Table 1. RETAIN weighting chart (Gunter et al., 2008, as seen in Prinsloo & Jordaan, 2014, p. 393)

		Level 0	Level 1	Level 2	Level 3
Relevance	1	0	1	2	3
Embedding	3	0	3	6	9
Transfer	5	0	5	10	15
Adaptation	4	0	4	8	12
Immersion	2	0	2	2	6
Naturalisation	6	0	6	12	18
Total possible points = 63					

This RETAIN rubric and its weighting chart was thus utilised to answer the first question, how does the assessment of the COTS SG named *Escape From Desolo* through the use of the RETAIN model justify the selection of the particular game for its use in English for shipping?

2.2. The four-dimensional framework

The four-dimensional framework of de Freitas and Oliver (2006) is for evaluating games and simulation-based education. It requires the practitioner to consider four main dimensions before using games and simulations in their practice in a way that all the aspects are related to each other and not considered individually (Ulicsak, 2010). In a nutshell, the four dimensions are as follows.

- "**Context:** which covers where the learning occurs – it includes the macro level, so historical, political, and economic factors (for example, are you playing because it is a school directive), through to micro, the tutor's background and experience, cost of game licences etc.

- **Learner Specification** for the individual or group – it requires the ESP instructor to consider their preferred learning style and previous knowledge and what methods would best support them given their differing needs.

- **Mode of Representation:** this includes the level of interactivity required, the fidelity, level of immersion produced. It also covers diegesis, the separation of the immersion aspect with the reflection around the process of playing the game. Most importantly it highlights the potential of briefing and debriefing to reinforce the learning outcomes.

- **Pedagogic principles:** these require the ESP instructor to reflect on the learning models which enable them to produce appropriate lesson plans" (De Freitas & Oliver, 2006, p. 260).

The framework was used to clarify the way the *Escape From Desolo* SG could be applied within the specific learning context by evaluating the pedagogic use of the tool, and not just the tool itself (De Freitas & Oliver, 2006) The aim was to answer the following questions.

- How does the dimension of the pedagogical considerations of the four-dimensional framework correspond to those of English for shipping?

- Which pedagogic approaches should be used to support learning outcomes and activities?

3. Results and discussion

3.1. The RETAIN model in Escape From Desolo

To assess how the *Escape From Desolo* COTS contains and incorporates academic content, the RETAIN aspects were calculated according to the weighting chart (Table 1 above). As proposed by Gunter et al. (2008), the aspects in the rubric were ordered according to their importance – from least to most important – as follows: relevance, immersion, embedding, adaptation, transfer, and naturalisation. This approach was adopted in the current paper as well. In fact, the lead researcher developed the weighting chart after playing and familiarising herself with the game.

Table 2. Resulting scores for Escape From Desolo

Element/Rating	Level x Rank = Rating
Relevance (2.5)	2.5 x 1 = 2.5 total pts
Embedding (3)	3 x 3 = 9 total pts
Transfer (2.5)	2.5 x 5 = 12.5 total pts
Adaptation (2.5)	2.5 x 4 = 10 total pts
Immersion (2)	2 x 2 = 4 total pts
Naturalisation (2)	2 x 6 = 12 total pts
Total:	50 / 63 pts

The table signifies each of the weighting aspects of the *Escape From Desolo* SG. Beginning with the least important, relevance (Rank 1), the resulting scores in

Table 2 revealed that the game has a strong relevance with the academic content (Rating : 2.5/3). Specifically, the focus of learning various onboard safety skills is evident in the game from the tutorial of the game, and it is designed in such a way that it is enjoyable to all ages, genders, or ranks. The *Escape From Desolo* SG is designed for prosperous seafarers/people wishing to work in the shipping industry. For this reason, the ESP learners will play the character/role of the young cadet who looks for a shore leave to meet his girlfriend. Yet, at points there is limited wording of the safety equipment, restricted to some snippets of information, probably based on the belief that the players have the knowledge already.

The game also provides moderately high levels of immersion (Rank 2) and naturalisation (Rank 6) because the game world creates a compelling fantasy for the player to be involved in cognitively and physically. The game mechanics such as sounds, graphic designs, and scenario based situations offer the opportunity for belief creation. Added to this, the players are psychologically and emotionally into the game content, as if they fail to do a good job, they will miss the opportunity to get a shore leave and thus meet Eve in Hamburg. Instant feedback loops, badges, progress bars, and leaderboards during each unit of the gameplay inform decisions of the players to reach their goal while adding to the pedagogy related mechanics.

As Table 3 reveals, *Escape From Desolo* embeds (Rank 3) relevant content at the highest level and therefore it was assigned with full points (nine total). Despite the partial lack of depth in educational content, the ability to play in a simulated ship environment provides the player with experiences of problems and contexts specific to the curriculum. The act of playing the game by moving around the simulated environment of the ship, while searching for clues to tackle situations, also builds up knowledge of the interior/exterior part of a ship while keeping players immersed in the fantasy context. Also, "the fantasy involves the learning material so much that players get to experience both simultaneously as if they are one (i.e. the educational content is fully endogenous to the fantasy context)" (Gunter et al., 2008, p. 517). However, "the challenge of the game is not based on increasingly difficult learning materials, but rather increasingly difficult game mechanics which are, though, not formed in discrete levels" (to be exact, there is a complete absence of levels) (Gunter et al., 2008, p. 533).

Chapter 7

Adaptation (Rank 4) received equally high scores with relevance and transfer of knowledge (Rank 5) because it allows for repetitive play through its varied content and fantasy context. As the player wanders across the simulated world of Desolo, he is repeatedly ventured into new, most of the time, risky situations. Learning thus becomes an active and participatory process in which the player builds upon what has already been learned in order to construct new ideas. In this manner, the player's way of thinking is improved, facilitating the need to look at how else acquired knowledge applies to the real world; a likely reason for this may be that the game world itself coincides so much with the academic context of safety at sea component of the English for shipping curriculum that players can easily understand the reason this knowledge may apply to a different context. The reason the game received a lower score for adaptation was due to the fact that the game provides the new content sequenced in such a way as to require players to identify old schema and transfer it to new ways of thinking.

The safety conventions, health/behaviour rules, and shipboard procedures deployed in the game are universal. Consequently, the principles learned from the game can easily be applied to other venues/countries and therefore facilitate the transfer of gained knowledge. Since the game features authentic real-life experiences – from responding to false abandon ship drills/fire alarms or emergencies of any kind to proper recycling of waste – active problem-solving is required to move to the next challenge. The very existence of experiences of this kind reward meaningful 'post event' knowledge acquisition, enforced with snippets of information that include facts about seafarers who, for instance, got injured or even died as a result of working at heights.

Going hand-in-hand with adaptation, the game features a wide spectrum of information for the player to utilise as he wanders in the different parts of the ship. The player is compelled to constantly revisit all that information in order for him to overcome future difficult conditions. As a result, players become more knowledgeable of everything they had previously found (this could be irritating/exhausting at parts). Yet, once the player has completed the game, there is little left to be accomplished. Repeated play is encouraged mostly to increase their scores on the international leaderboard; still, there is no variation offered "with regards to adding curiosity or novelty to practice. Replaying the game does not add anything new for the player other than perform the same game over for the same knowledge – possibly acting as a refresher, but with little motivation to do so, once the novelty wears off" (Gunter et al., 2008, p. 532).

Overall, with the use of the RETAIN model, the game received 50 points out of a total of 63.

3.2. The four-dimensional framework in Escape From Desolo

The four-dimensional framework was used to evaluate the potential use of *Escape For Desolo* as part of the specific ESP curriculum (De Freitas & Oliver, 2006). The authors proposed a table of focus to help practitioners estimate properly the four dimensions/aspects of games before their implementation and thus anticipate particular issues. Employing this table, the authors show the way it has been used to evaluate the *Escape From Desolo* SG as illustrated in Table 3.

Table 3. Using the four-dimensional framework to evaluate Escape For Desolo

Context	Learner Specification	Pedagogical Considerations	Mode of Representation (tools for use)
School-based learning in English for shipping studies/ commerce, finance, and shipping studies.	School learners 22-26 years old, undergraduate students of commerce, finance, and shipping, at CUT. The learners are familiar with the context of safety at sea as they have attended related classes over their studies but in the Greek language.	"Use of theories such as Kolb's (1984) Experiential learning where learners learn from experience through abstract conceptualisation and application into practice might be effective" (De Freitas & Oliver, 2006, p. 261).	Escape From Desolo uses a medium of fidelity based upon the use of 3D animated characters.

Chapter 7

Interactions with the software via the students own mobile phone/ easy installation/ no further need for technical support after it is downloaded and installed/ Free access.	The tool is currently been used for training the prospect seafarers on onboard safety skills in classroom but it can be used by all ages, ranks, and genders.	Curricula objectives include safety at sea conventions (MARPOL- International Convention for the Prevention of Pollution from Ships, SOLAS-Safety of Life at Sea, and STWC- International Convention on Standards of Training, Certification, and Watchkeeping for Seafarers) and safety issues including overloading, collision, fire, and (personal) protective equipment. Learning outcomes: conversancy with onboard difficulties (interior/exterior part of the ship) and approaches allowing the students to experience emergency conditions/situations onboard first-hand and learn how to anticipate them.	Escape From Desolo "uses a high level of interactivity between the media world and the learners' own experiences and knowledge, allowing the student to develop an increasing conservancy with the rules and functionality of the simulation tool" (De Freitas & Oliver, 2006, p. 261).
Escape from Desolo supports safety at sea components of the English for shipping curriculum. It can support classroom-based practical teaching/learning or even informal learning due to its aforementioned specifications.	The tool can be used by learners working only singly, not in groups, due to its single story driven nature. Therefore, teacher-led instruction of the related academic context should be preceded.	Learning activities: the student learns through tasks based upon problem-solving situations of safety onboard.	Learning activities and outcomes achieved through specially developed software supporting an increased awareness of the learner of the processes of reaction in emergency situations and emergency drilling through increased usage.

	"Range of differentiated learners with different learning styles can be catered to through the use of this tool as each learner can engage with the resource according to their own preferences" (De Freitas & Oliver, 2006, p. 261).	Briefing/Debriefing: pre-class preparation and post activity reflection and consideration.	
		"Simulation embedded as a practical session into the lesson plan of the tutor. Individuals will need different levels of attention from the tutor at different stages of the learning process" (De Freitas & Oliver, 2006, p. 261).	

Completing the table, the game design and its possible pedagogic use are highlighted. Regarding the context, it is obvious that *Escape From Desolo* specifications serve for both classroom-based implementation as well as at home use; hence, the learners may want to practise using the tool in the home context as well, supporting informal as well as formal learning processes and thus, reinforcing learning. In both situations, it may be applied as a practical tool; a tool that serves for practical experience of safety onboard skills. It is particularly interesting that it may be used by anyone, regardless of gender, age, or rank. Due to its nature, all types of learners may engage with the tool, yet prior knowledge of the academic content is necessary. Therefore, the tutors should consider some pedagogical challenges in advance to the game's integration. In particular, the table highlights the pedagogic models and approaches that are needed to embed *Escape From Desolo* into effective practice. In this particular context, "experiential learning (Kolb, 1984) might be used to support the cyclical transition from abstract conceptualisation towards concrete action and reflection. The table also enables a deeper reflection of the ESP instructor as to whether the tool can be used to support informal as well as curricula led consideration' (De Freitas & Oliver, 2006, p. 262).

A notable strength of *Escape From Desolo* is that it is designed alongside the international conventions and laws of the maritime Studies which shape the duties onboard and/or how to react in an emergency situation or even in false alarms. This allows for a closer fit with the English for shipping curriculum component of safety at sea; a key consideration for ESP instructors wishing to embed games and simulations into teaching practice.

4. Conclusion

This case study intended to explore current evaluation techniques and tools relevant in clarifying the characteristics of the *Escape From Desolo* SG integration into an ESP curriculum. From the analysis of the data collected from the tools employed, it was evident that the *Escape From Desolo* COTS SG could be applied in the English for shipping curriculum and specifically as part of the safety at sea component. Not only the close relevance of the academic content but also the high levels of immersion, naturalisation, and adaptation of the fantasy/story content were considered primarily for the validation and the selection of the curriculum component it could be integrated into. The fact that the academic content was so highly embedded in the fantasy story of the game enables players/learners to use the game as an opportunity for experiential learning or learning-by-doing. Facing simulated difficulties onboard which are stimulated by the game mechanics can emerge real-life situations that would be difficult for the ESP instructor to bring into the classroom otherwise. This element may also add to the level of the player's attention into the game as they are trying to find solutions to the occurring situations. In fact, these emergency situations, which revolve around the story-driven nature of the gameplay, can be thought of as a reinforcing relationship between the player and the sequence of events of the gameplay. They work as a snowball – something that starts up as a small part and gets larger as it happens over and over again. They grow over the use of the feedback loops and/or progress bars. The very existence of feedback loops and progress bars as game mechanics enables the players to put emphasis on the early game, since the effects of the early game are magnified over time. They thus eliminate the teacher led instructions during the gameplay and provide the player with the opportunity of learning the academic content by playing. It also provides the player with the opportunity to revise and thus enhance prior acquired knowledge. Yet, the story driven nature of the game does not include discrete levels of the game. This absence of integrated levels within gameplay allows room for consideration on behalf of the ESP instructor regarding the best way to implement the game, at which particular part of the in-class lesson, and for how long the players should use it in order to keep them interested to carry on playing. The specifications of the game regarding its cost free nature, the no-limit age, or gender group that it addresses were proven highly valuable. Although the free mobile access is considered an advantage, prior to the implementation the instructor should consider the system of the phones each student occupies as the software is only available on Android and not iOS. Finally, the single user/ learner specification of the game requires prior class preparation with teacher-led instruction of the related content and post activity reflection and consideration regarding the added value of the game as a teaching practice.

This chapter has examined the decisions instructors should take before embedding a SG in formal education. The authors have proposed an approach to SG evaluation that draws inspiration from the principles of the RETAIN framework and the four-dimensional framework. These were adopted in the single-case study design research of *Escape From Desolo* COTS SG in an attempt to examine and share some fundamental issues arising from the enactment of experimental activities in formal education contexts. The results from the case study, although limited to a specific ESP context, could prove useful and could be applied in different contexts for future studies. Finally, we should highlight here that this paper constitutes the pre-implementation evaluation of the *Escape From Desolo* SG. An analytic description of the *Escape From Desolo* SG implementation will be provided in a future paper.

Chapter 7

Acknowledgements

We would like to thank the participants of this study.

References

Aldrich, C. (2009). *The complete guide to simulations and serious games: how the most valuable content will be created in the age beyond Gutenberg to Google.* John Wiley & Sons.

Arnab, S., Berta, R., Earp, J., De Freitas, S., Popescu, M., Romero, M., ..., & Usart, M. (2012). Framing the adoption of serious games in formal education. *Electronic Journal of E-Learning, 10*(2), 159-171.

Baldauf, M., Schröder-Hinrichs, J.-U., Kataria, A., Benedict, K., & Tuschling, G. (2016). Multidimensional simulation in team training for safety and security in maritime transportation. *Journal of Transportation Safety & Security, 8*(3), 197-213.

Care, E., Kim, H., Vista, A., & Anderson, K. (2018). *Education system alignment for 21st century skills: focus on assessment.* Center for Universal Education at The Brookings Institution, 1775 Massachusettes Avenue NW, Washington, DC 20036.

David, M. M., & Watson, A. (2008). Participating in what? Using situated cognition theory to illuminate differences in classroom practices. In A. Watson & P. Winbourne (Eds), *New directions for situated cognition in mathematics education* (pp. 31-57). Springer. https://doi.org/10.1007/978-0-387-71579-7_3

De Freitas, S., & Oliver, M. (2006). How can exploratory learning with games and simulations within the curriculum be most effectively evaluated? *Computers & Education, 46*(3), 249-264. https://doi.org/10.1016/j.compedu.2005.11.007

Djaouti, D., Alvarez, J., Jessel, J.-P., & Rampnoux, O. (2011). Origins of serious games. In M. Ma, A. Oikonomou & L. C. Jain (Eds), *Serious games and edutainment applications* (pp. 25-43). Springer. https://doi.org/10.1007/978-1-4471-2161-9_3

Djuraskovic, I., & Arthur, N. (2010). Heuristic inquiry: a personal journey of acculturation and identity reconstruction. *Qualitative Report, 15*(6), 1569-1593.

Gunter, G. A., Kenny, R. F., & Vick, E. H. (2008). Taking educational games seriously: using the RETAIN model to design endogenous fantasy into standalone educational games. *Educational Technology Research and Development, 56*(5-6), 511-537. https://doi.org/10.1007/s11423-007-9073-2

Hutchinson, T., & Waters, A. (1987). *English for specific purposes.* Cambridge University Press.

Karshenas, S., & Haber, D. (2012). Developing a serious game for construction planning and scheduling education. In *Construction Research Congress 2012: Construction Challenges in a Flat World* (pp. 2042-2051). https://doi.org/10.1061/9780784412329.205

Kocdar, S., Okur, M., & Bozkurt, A. (2017). An Examination of xMOOCs: an embedded single case study based on Conole's 12 dimensions. *Turkish Online Journal of Distance Education, 18*(4), 52-65. https://doi.org/10.17718/tojde.340381

Kolb, D. A. (1984). *Experiential learning: experience as the source of learning and development.* Prentice-Hall.

Michael, D. R., & Chen, S. L. (2005). *Serious games: games that educate, train, and inform.* Muska & Lipman/Premier-Trade.

Prinsloo, J. W., & Jordaan, D. B. (2014). Selecting serious games for the computer science class. *Mediterranean Journal of Social Sciences, 5*(21), 391-398. https://doi.org/10.5901/mjss.2014.v5n21p391

Robertson, S. L. (2019). Interactive digital instruction: pedagogy of the 21st century classroom. In *Handbook of research on promoting higher-order skills and global competencies in life and work* (pp. 166-180). IGI Global. https://doi.org/10.4018/978-1-5225-6331-0.ch011

Schreiber, J. B., & Asner-Self, K. (2011). *The interrelationship of questions, sampling, design, and analysis.* Wiley & Sons.

Ulicsak, M. (2010). *Games in education: serious games-a futurelab literature review.* https://www.nfer.ac.uk/publications/FUTL60/FUTL60.pdf

Vintimilla-Tapia, P. E., Peñafiel-Vicuña, C. J., Bravo-Torres, J. F., Gallegos-Segovia, P. L., Yuquilima-Albarado, I. F., & Ordónez-Morales, E. F. (2018). A multi-subject serious game as an education tool: analysis from the teacher's perspective. In *2018 IEEE Biennial Congress of Argentina (ARGENCON)* (pp. 1-7). https://doi.org/10.1109/argencon.2018.8646131

Yin, R. K. (1994). Discovering the future of the case study. Method in evaluation research. *Evaluation Practice, 15*(3), 283-290. https://doi.org/10.1016/0886-1633(94)90023-x

Zyda, M. (2005). From visual simulation to virtual reality to games. *Computer, 38*(9), 25-32. https://doi.org/10.1109/mc.2005.297

8. Facilitating the development of collaborative online dictionaries in the ESP field

Eleni Nikiforou[1]

Abstract

The English for Specific Purposes (ESP) field is currently receiving a lot of attention as researchers and practitioners seek to improve the learning experience for the students and raise the quality of the courses. To advance ESP practice, it is crucial that teacher training in ESP is enhanced and supported through exemplary practices. Vocabulary development is established as a central trait in ESP, yet it still poses a challenging aspect of the teaching practice. This chapter discusses a specific vocabulary task through which guidance is provided to teachers in order to facilitate the development of ESP vocabulary in their ESP teaching contexts. This research reports on the results of data collected from a course in a tertiary institution in Cyprus where ESP students worked collaboratively to create an online biomedical dictionary on a wiki. The research conducted is qualitative, and grounded theory was applied. Finally, this chapter concludes with certain criteria which afford the application of this vocabulary enhancement task in any ESP and English as a Foreign Language (EFL) course across different language levels as well as in mixed ability classrooms.

Keywords: ESP, online dictionary, collaboration, wiki, teacher training.

1. University of Cyprus, Nicosia, Cyprus; eleninik@ucy.ac.cy; https://orcid.org/0000-0002-3603-5091

How to cite this chapter: Nikiforou, E. (2019). Facilitating the development of collaborative online dictionaries in the ESP field. In S. Papadima-Sophocleous, E. Kakoulli Constantinou & C. N. Giannikas (Eds), *ESP teaching and teacher education: current theories and practices* (pp. 131-146). Research-publishing.net. https://doi.org/10.14705/rpnet.2019.33.930

Chapter 8

1. Introduction

One of the key aspects of ESP teaching is the enhancement of the students' vocabulary in the specific area they are studying. Dudley-Evans (1998) includes vocabulary as one of the absolute characteristics for ESP: "ESP is centered on the language appropriate to these activities in terms of grammar, lexis, register, study skills, discourse and genre" (p. 6). Further to this, vocabulary learning is often viewed as a challenge for language learners (Akbarian, 2010; Coxhead, 2013; Weil, 2008). To enhance the development of ESP vocabulary, language instructors need to design tasks and use information technology tools that support the learning process (Chen, Doong, & Hsu, 2013; Ching, 2012). This chapter illustrates a specific vocabulary task that ESP instructors can apply in their language classrooms in order to enhance the learning of new ESP vocabulary items. It discusses aspects of the design and administration of the specific vocabulary task in order to enable the discussion of those conditions that need to be met for the task to be used effectively in ESP courses. The task may be transferable to other ESP courses and it can be adjusted to suit different levels of language learning.

More specifically, this chapter looks at the variety of contributions made by students on a wiki in order to create their own biomedical dictionary in an English for Biomedical Sciences course offered to undergraduate students of the University of Cyprus so that the discussion on how teachers can apply the task is afforded.

A wiki is an online tool that has the features of a website and allows multiple users to collaborate "allowing any user to add and edit content" (Oxford Dictionary[2]). The wiki as a tool is distinctive because of its "dynamic and constantly changing web-based environments" (Aydin, 2014, p. 208). There are multiple studies that support the use of the wiki for collaborative language learning (Bradley, Lindstrom, & Rystedt, 2010; Kessler & Bikowski, 2010; Matthew, Felvegi, & Callaway, 2009).

---

2. https://en.oxforddictionaries.com/definition/wiki

The majority of the studies on the use of wikis in language classrooms focus on the improvement of writing skills through collaboration (Arnold, Ducate, & Kost, 2009; Bradley et al., 2010; Li, 2012; Wang, 2015). No research studies were found that focus specifically on the development of vocabulary skills with the use of wikis. In fact, Kilickaya and Krajka (2010), in a study about the teachers' technology use in vocabulary teaching, found out that the wiki is rarely used for vocabulary development. However, the development of vocabulary skills is mentioned in a few studies as a skill that can also be improved through the wiki application in the language learning classroom (Carney-Strahler, 2011; Wiseman & Belknap, 2013).

2. Methodology

2.1. Context

The course, English for Biomedical Sciences, as an ESP course followed a student-centred approach, taking into consideration the learner-needs and the context. Furthermore, the course also applied blended learning, collaborative learning, and task-based language learning methodologies.

Data was collected from the completion of a vocabulary task that involved the students working collaboratively to create an online biomedical dictionary on a wiki, for which the free version of pbworks wiki was used. The wiki was password-protected; therefore, only the students taking the specific course, and their instructor, had access to it. The instructor introduced the task in-class and gave the guidelines which entailed the addition of three vocabulary items (in alphabetical order) on the wiki dictionary page approximately once a week during the 13-week semester. Further to this, the students were informed that this task was not graded. The task commenced in Week 2 and continued to Week 13.

This task was designed to support a variety of activities and projects that were included in the course syllabus. The words added to the dictionary were selected by the students from the course authentic online material as well as material from books used for reading, listening, writing, and speaking tasks. For example, students added words in their online dictionary after reading an article, completing a listening task, and researching sources for their scientific poster presentation. The students were asked to provide a definition, as well as an example sentence for each vocabulary item. They were also encouraged to offer more information such as pronunciation guides for each lexical item, word parts, pictures, and videos, but this was optional.

Students were required to enter new words in the dictionary that had not been already added by their peers. This supported scaffolding of the vocabulary level of difficulty as the students chose the vocabulary items based on their own individual language level and language competency. As well as learner autonomy, as they were in control of selecting the vocabulary items for the wiki.

2.2. Participants

There were 29 participating students in the study. They were first and second year undergraduate students from the Department of Biological Sciences. There were 21 female and eight male students. Although descriptors at Common European Framework of Reference for languages (CEFR) level B2 are embedded in the course syllabus, the actual level of the students, as indicated by a diagnostic test given at the beginning of the semester, was mixed ability, varying from A2 to C1.

2.3. Grounded theory approach

This research project followed a grounded theory approach, which is defined as the "discovery of theory from data" (Glazer & Strauss, 2009, p. 1). Grounded theory has an "inductive but systematic approach to design and data analysis" (Gray, 2009, p. 171) as the theories derive through the analysis of rich data (Charmaz, 2006, p. 14). The application of this approach enables surfacing concepts to initiate further research in the area. In this research project, the retrospective quality of grounded theory helps the researcher gain a good insight into the learning processes that occur. In addition to this, it facilitates the development of specific criteria that teachers need to follow in order to transfer this task to their own professional practice.

An integral part of grounded theory is coding, as it helps in the "conceptualization of data" (Holton, 2007, p. 238). In this research project, the emergent themes were identified in a comparative analysis, which in turn enabled the formation of the three categories (student collaboration, frequency of participation in the task, quality of participation in the task) as discussed in the data analysis section below.

The collected data were analysed and coded following the principles of grounded theory. The wiki history page provided most of the data for this research project. Furthermore, student questionnaires (n=29) and three student semi-structured interviews offered a valuable insight on diverse aspects of the task and afforded the triangulation of results.

3. Data analysis

The history of the wiki page was coded to allow for themes to emerge following the guidelines of grounded theory. The transcripts of the interviews were coded and analysed, focussing on similarities and differences so that themes could surface. Finally, the student questionnaires were analysed using Microsoft Office Excel Spreadsheets because of the small number of questions and participants. The themes that derived from the data analysis were translated into the following three categories as shown in Table 1 below:

- student collaboration to complete the task;

- student frequency of participation in the task; and

- student quality of participation in the task.

Table 1. Data analysis

Source	Themes	Categories
• Wiki history page • Wiki page • Questionnaire and interviews	• Student involvement in other people's entries • Outcome of the task • Motivation • Student collaboration • Addition of vocabulary items • Editing other students' work • Maintaining the appearance of the wiki dictionary page	• Student collaboration
• Wiki history page • Interviews	• Number of student revisions on the wiki page • Dates of students' edits on the wiki page • Time spent on the task • Frequency of additions and revisions	• Frequency of student participation
• Wiki history page • Wiki page • Questionnaire and interviews	• Formatting: changes to the font colour, font size, italics, bold letters • Media: pictures and videos • Editing: surface mistakes (typographical errors, spelling mistakes, and grammar mistakes) • Paraphrasing: rewriting and meaning changes • Outcome of the task • Kinds of revisions • Motivation	• Quality of student participation

4. Results and discussion

4.1. Collaboration

Data analysis indicated that the students collaborated to enter vocabulary items and to make meaning changes in the online dictionary. The wiki history page demonstrated that all students (n=29) added different vocabulary items from each other, and most of them (n=24) edited the words added. Student interviews support the above findings. A theme that derived from all three interviews was that the students spent some time to confirm that the words they planned to add had not already been entered on the online dictionary. This was an indication that the students collaborated by assuming responsibility for the definition of different terms. This is an indicator that the dictionary development, in relation to the variety of the word items added, was the result of student collaboration.

Furthermore, the students collaborated to format and edit vocabulary items as well as to add pictures and videos as reflected on the wiki history page. The history page showed that 17 students improved spelling mistakes or surface grammatical errors in other students' vocabulary items. Approximately half the students (n=15) also added pictures or videos to each other's word entries. It is interesting to note that the number of students (n=13) who had originally added the vocabulary items noticed these additions and revised what their classmates added to their word entries by making mainly formatting changes. The results from the student questionnaires also confirm that to a great extent students collaborated to improve the entries on the online dictionary in the areas of media, formatting, editing, and to a lesser extent they collaborated to improve the meaning of those entries by paraphrasing (see Table 2 below).

4.2. Frequency of participation

The students started to enter and edit their vocabulary items in Week 2. There was a radical increase in Week 4 in the number of times the students edited the online dictionary (see Figure 1 below). The analysis of the data from the wiki

Chapter 8

page illustrated that the students added not only definitions and examples of the vocabulary items, but also pictures and videos. They also made formatting changes.

Figure 1. Arabic 1 frequency of participation

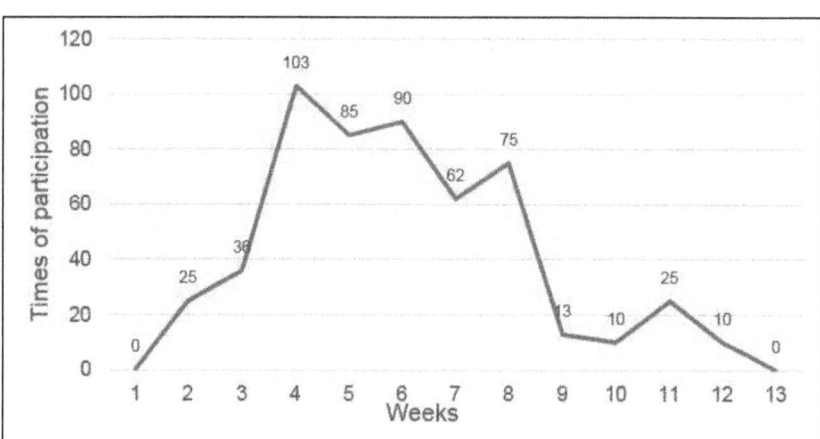

As reflected on the wiki history page, four students added pictures and videos on the wiki during Week 3. This seems to have motivated the majority of the students (n=22) to revisit their vocabulary items to add pictures and videos as it was evident on the wiki history page in Weeks 4 and 5. This was an indication that the students were interested in the outcome of the dictionary, and it also illustrated that the students wanted to offer consistent and coherent information for the word entries.

The frequency of participation remained high with only a significant decrease in Week 9 when the students took their midterm exam as they were not required to add words in the wiki. It is also noteworthy that after Week 10 the students were not assigned any specific homework in relation to this task, so any additions and/or edits were their own initiatives. When asked in the student interviews on whether they visited the online dictionary and worked on it after Week 10, the students' responses showed different points of view:

"I did not put [sic] anything, but I visited the dictionary to see it again. We did not have homework, so I don't work but I got an email [from pbworks] about changes and want [sic] to see them" (Student 1).

"I wanted to add vocabulary because it was fun" (Student 2).

"I didn't add words, but I uploaded pictures for two words that I put in the past" (Student 3).

4.3. Quality of participation

While examining the kind of modifications that the students did on the wiki page, as well as their responses to the questionnaire and student interviews, four themes surfaced that relate to the quality of their work (see Table 1 above):

- formatting: changes to the font colour, font size, italics, bold, etc.;

- media: addition and deletion of pictures and/or videos;

- editing: surface mistakes such as typographical errors, spelling mistakes, and grammar mistakes; and

- paraphrasing: rewriting the items using their own words and meaning changes (see Figure 2 below).

More than half of the changes (53%) that took place after the items were added on the wiki related to format changes. Format changes included modifications to the colour or the size of the fonts, capitalisation, use of italics, or bold letters. This percentage indicates that the students spent time taking care of the appearance of the wiki page. This is also supported by their responses in Question 7 and Question 8 in the questionnaire as shown in Table 2 below. From the student responses in the interviews, it was evident that the students' formatting changes stemmed from a variety of incentives. It seems that certain students might have found it easier to deal with formatting changes, others were interested in improving the appearance because this would enhance the learning process, and other students might have edited for their own personal reasons:

> "It's easy to change letters...um...the colour...so I help this in the wiki" (Student 1).
>
> "I wanted the dictionary to look good so it was easy to find the words" (Student 2).
>
> "I have OCD, I wanted to fix everything" (Student 3).

As only three students were interviewed, there cannot be a generalisation regarding formatting changes but nevertheless, it is an indication as to how the students approached the task.

Figure 2. Arabic 2 quality of participation

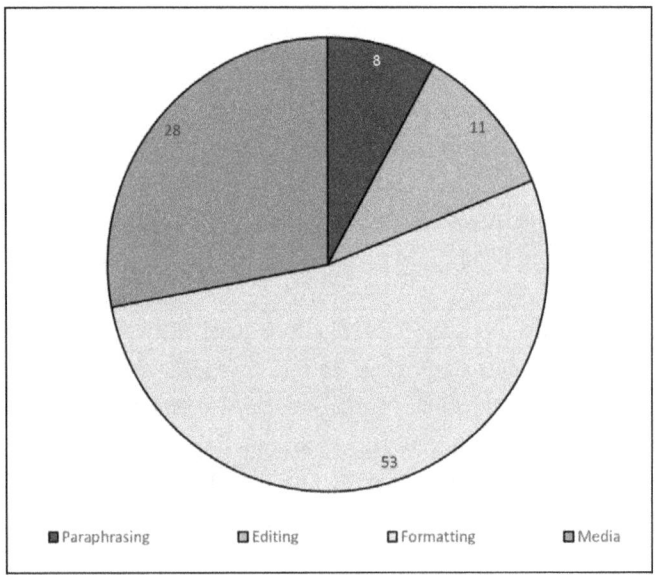

Another percentage (28%) related to the media uploaded on the wiki, which included both adding and/or deleting pictures and videos or changing the pictures and/or videos. This percentage increased in Weeks 3 and 4 after four students added the first pictures and videos in Week 2. This was an indication that they may have found the media useful in the understanding of the vocabulary items. This was also supported by all three student interviews as the students stated that the use of media helps them "understand difficult words" (Student 1), "made the definition of the words complete" (Student 2), and "help illustrate the meaning" (Student 3). It is interesting to note that five students returned to delete already existing videos and pictures and add new ones in different word items as shown on the history page of the wiki. A reason for this was provided by Student 3 in the interview, as they pointed out that they "deleted videos and found better ones to explain the words". The replies to Question 3 and Question 4 relating to the media in the questionnaires also agree with the findings from the wiki and the interviews (see Table 2).

The students (11%) improved editing issues on the online dictionary including surface mistakes such as spelling mistakes, typos, and grammar mistakes as well. Surface mistakes were corrected once and students did not come back to them which explains the low percentage of changes. The majority of the students supported that they edited their work (nu.=16 agree or strongly agree) and other students' work on the wiki (n=21) as shown in the results of the student questionnaire in Table 2.

Only 8% of the changes related to paraphrasing and rewriting the items using their own words. This was not surprising for the researcher, as the students were introduced to paraphrasing later in the semester whereas the online dictionary was developed in the beginning of the semester. However, this percentage indicates only the changes that occurred after the items were added to the dictionary. This means that they could have already been paraphrased upon their addition to the dictionary. Student questionnaires showed that approximately half the students (n=15) edited their own entries for meaning and only four students edited other students' work for meaning (see Table 2).

Chapter 8

Furthermore, it is noteworthy that each vocabulary item was formed by accumulating information from different sources as the actual wiki page showed, for example for the definition of the word *meiosis* the students used an online dictionary for the pronunciation guide and word part, Wikipedia for the definition, and YouTube for a video that explains the word. The students used a variety of sources in researching and writing the information for each vocabulary item as the end-result illustrated on the online dictionary. This was also supported from the student questionnaire, as 28 students strongly agreed that they used two or more sources to collect information before adding work on the online dictionary (see Table 2).

Data from the questionnaire, in an open-ended question on the student's opinion on the task, indicated that the students found the development of the online dictionary: 'useful' (n=19), 'motivating' (n=26), 'fun' (n=13), 'easy' (n=27), 'interesting' (n=22), 'worthwhile' (n=9), and 'appropriate' (n=4). Further research is necessary to indicate as to why the students attributed these characteristics to the task and to confirm the hypothesis that results from the use of these adjectives.

Table 2. Questionnaire results

Question	Strongly disagree	Disagree	Neither agree or disagree	Agree	Strongly agree
Overall, I enjoyed working on the online dictionary task.			2	15	12
I added three words every week.				2	27
I added media (pictures and/or videos) to the words I added.			2		27
I added media (pictures and/ or videos) to the words other students added.		7	4	13	5
I edited the words I added.		10	3	15	1
I edited other students' words.		5	3	20	1
I changed the colours, the fonts, italics on the dictionary of the words I added.			2		27

I changed the colours, the fonts, italics on the dictionary of the words other students added.		6	3	8	12
I corrected/edited the meaning of the words I added.		12	2	14	1
I corrected/edited the meaning of the words other students added.	8	14	3	3	1
I collected information from only one source.		27	2		
I collected information from two or more sources.			1		28

5. Conclusions

It should be noted that the specific task was perceived as effective since the students spent time working with ESP vocabulary items and created their own ESP dictionary. However, the application of the grounded theory approach in the project, which is inductive in nature, facilitated only the students' perspectives to surface from the data analysis.

The data were collected and analysed from the specific context, course, and students offering the student perspective; therefore, generalisations should be avoided. More research would enable a greater insight in the task to establish the actual learning outcomes resulting from the specific task. Further to this, the task should be repeated in different contexts in order to confirm the results of this research project and evaluate the characteristics suggested below.

As mentioned above, the specific task enabled the students to work with vocabulary and to create their own artefact. For such a task to work in language rooms, we need to apply the characteristics that increased its effectiveness and can potentially make the task transferrable to other language learning contexts.

The following task characteristics are likely to have contributed to the effectiveness of the task:

- ownership: the students felt that they were creating an artefact that belonged to them and they wanted to make sure that it was coherent, effective, and engaging;

- scaffolding: the students were able to contribute to the task to the extent of their abilities – the weak students could contribute with easier words and the stronger students with more challenging vocabulary;

- autonomous learning: the students were given control over the content and they were encouraged to assume responsibility for their learning;

- safe environment: the wiki was password-protected so only students taking the course could access the dictionary; and

- task rationale: the students could relate to the rationale behind the task which motivated them to add the vocabulary items and to edit them.

These characteristics that have afforded the enhancement of vocabulary skills in ESP courses may be used as criteria for the successful application of the task in other teaching contexts. With careful planning and introduction, this task can be successfully transferred to a variety of contexts, content subjects, and levels. Language practitioners can use this task in their ESP courses to further enhance the development of ESP technical vocabulary. Further research is recommended to identify how the students respond to this type of task in order to further improve its implementation in the language learning classroom and other ESP contexts.

References

Akbarian, I. (2010). The relationship between vocabulary size and depth for ESP/EAP learners. *System, 38*(3), 391-401. https://doi.org/10.1016/j.system.2010.06.013

Arnold, N., Ducate, L., & Kost, C. (2009). Collaborative writing in wikis. In L. Lomicka & G. Lord (Eds), *The next generation: social networking and online collaboration in foreign language learning*. CALICO Monograph Series, *8*, 115-144.

Aydin, S. (2014). Wikis as a tool for collaborative language learning: implications for literacy, language education and multilingualism. *Sustainable Multilingualism*, 5, 207-236. https://doi.org/10.7220/2335-2027.5.8

Bradley, L., Lindstrom, B., & Rystedt, H. (2010). Rationalities of collaboration for language learning in a wiki. *ReCALL, 22*(2), 247-265. https://doi.org/10.1017/s0958344010000108

Carney-Strahler, B. (2011). Wikis: promoting collaborative literacy through affordable technology in content-area classrooms. *Creative Education, 2*(2), 76-82. https://doi.org/10.4236/ce.2011.22011

Charmaz, K. (2006). *Constructing grounded theory: a practical guide through qualitative analysis*. SAGE publications.

Chen, Y. L., Doong, J. L., & Hsu, C. C. (2013). Contextualized vocabulary learning through a virtual learning environment. In R. McBride & M. Searson (Eds), *Proceedings of SITE 2013--Society for Information Technology & Teacher Education International Conference* (pp. 4108-4114). Association for the Advancement of Computing in Education (AACE). https://www.learntechlib.org/primary/p/48764/

Ching, G. (2012). Blog assisted learning: experiences in learning business English vocabularies. *International Journal of Research Studies in Educational Technology IJRSET, 1*(1), 3-12. https://doi.org/10.5861/ijrset.2012.v1i1.10

Coxhead, A. (2013). Vocabulary and ESP. In B. Paltridge & S. Starfield (Eds), *The handbook of English for specific purposes* (pp. 115-132). Wiley. https://doi.org/10.1002/9781118339855.ch6

Dudley-Evans, T. (1998). *An overview of ESP in the 1990s*. The Japan Conference on English for Specific Purposes Proceedings.

Glazer, B. G., & Strauss, A. L. (2009). *The discovery of grounded theory: strategies for qualitative research*. Transaction Publishers.

Gray, D. E. (2009). *Doing research in the real world*. SAGE publications.

Holton, J. (2007). The coding process and its challenges. In A. Bryant & K. Charmaz (Eds), *The Sage handbook of grounded theory*. SAGE publications.

Kessler, G., & Bikowski, D. (2010). Developing collaborative autonomous learning abilities in computer mediated language learning: attention to meaning among students in wiki space. *Computer Assisted Language Learning, 23*(1), 41-58. https://doi.org/10.1080/09588220903467335

Kilickaya, F., & Krajka, J. (2010). Teachers' technology use in vocabulary teaching. *Academic Exchange Quarterly*, 81-86.

Li, M. (2012). Use of wikis in second/foreign language classes: a literature review. *CALL-EJ, 13*(1), 17-35.

Matthew, K. I., Felvegi, E., & Callaway, R. A. (2009). Wiki as a collaborative learning tool in a language arts methods class. *Journal of Research on Technology in Education, 42*(1), 51-72. https://doi.org/10.1080/15391523.2009.10782541

Wang, Y.-C. (2015). Promoting collaborative writing through wikis: a new approach for advancing innovative and active learning in an ESP context. *Computer Assisted Language Learning, 28*(6), 499-512. https://doi.org/10.1080/09588221.2014.881386

Weil, N. (2008). Vocabulary size, background characteristics, and reading skill of Korean intensive English. *The Asian EFL Journal Quarterly: Conference Proceedings, 10*(4), 26-59.

Wiseman, C. S., & Belknap, J. P. (2013). Wikis: a knowledge platform for collaborative learning in ESL reading. *TESOL Journal, 4*(2), 360-369. https://doi.org/10.1002/tesj.83

9. Going beyond words and actions: teaching metacognitive and soft skills to ESP communication students at the dawn of the fourth industrial revolution

Dana Di Pardo Léon-Henri[1]

Abstract

One of the fundamental objectives of education is to teach lifelong learning skills that will help people navigate through their careers and future relationships towards both personal and professional fulfilment. Educators would then not only teach the core subjects and hard skills, but they would also need to focus on teaching soft skills, which are both valuable to and revered by 21st century professionals. Excellent verbal and non-verbal communication skills make up a significant part of these soft skills, which are transversal and take the form of people skills or sociability. The focus of this chapter is to examine the ways in which new technologies can be integrated into reflective English for Specific Purposes (ESP) teaching methods to stimulate student motivation and encourage the development of the aforementioned skills which are not only professional, but also metacognitive in nature, within the context of first year non-specialist English language students in Communication Studies. The chapter begins by presenting the scholarship and theoretical framework for a Student-Centred Learning (SCL) approach and procedures for a collaborative One-Minute Film Project. Finally, it presents some initial positive results based on the data, as well as various observations and potential for further transversal research.

---

1. Université de Franche-Comté, Besançon, France; danaleonhenri@gmail.com; https://orcid.org/0000-0001-6196-6173

How to cite this chapter: Di Pardo Léon-Henri, D. (2019). Going beyond words and actions: teaching metacognitive and soft skills to ESP communication students at the dawn of the fourth industrial revolution. In S. Papadima-Sophocleous, E. Kakoulli Constantinou & C. N. Giannikas (Eds), *ESP teaching and teacher education: current theories and practices* (pp. 147-161). Research-publishing.net. https://doi.org/10.14705/rpnet.2019.33.931

Chapter 9

Keywords: fourth industrial revolution, ESP, language pedagogy, metacognitive skills, soft skills, student-centred learning, verbal communication, non-verbal communication.

1. Introduction

We are at the dawn of the Fourth Industrial Revolution (FIR), and as Klaus Schwab (2016), Founder and Executive Chairman of the World Economic Forum stated, we are on the brink of a technological revolution that has already begun to fundamentally alter the way we live, work, and relate to one another. Today's highly mobile and rapidly evolving technology dependent society has created a work force of individuals who have radically changed over the years. This trend will continue as billions of people connected by mobile devices encounter emerging breakthroughs in fields such as artificial intelligence and robotics, for example. Accordingly, the required professional skills and qualities of future job candidates is swiftly evolving since "over one third of skills (35%) that are considered important in today's workforce will have changed […] by 2020"[2] (Gray, 2016, n.p.).

Schwab (2016) also maintains that "[l]ike the revolutions that preceded it, the Fourth Industrial Revolution has the potential to raise global income levels and improve the quality of life for populations around the world [but at] the same time, [it] could [potentially] yield greater inequality, particularly in its potential to disrupt labour markets[, as] automation [i.e. robotics] substitutes for labour" (n.p.). Understandably, many blue-collar and middle class workers have and will continue to become "disillusioned and fearful that their own […] incomes and those [perhaps] of their children will continue to stagnate" (Schwab, 2016, n.p.) or dwindle in light of such drastic societal changes. This is especially true if one is a technophobe or does not possess computer or smartphone savvy in the 21st century.

---

2. For more precise information on how these skills have changed, refer to the supplementary materials, Appendix 1, Figure 1 'Top Ten Skills: 2020 vs. 2015' or refer to the report 'The Future of Jobs' (pp. 21-22) at the following link http://www3.weforum.org/docs/WEF_Future_of_Jobs.pdf

1.1. The FIR and the ESP Language Classroom

The FIR is inevitably changing

> "not only what we do, but also who we are, since it profoundly affects our identity and all the issues associated with it: our sense of privacy, our notions of ownership, our consumption patterns, the time we devote to work and leisure, and how we develop our careers, cultivate our skills, meet people, and nurture relationships" (Schwab, 2016, n.p.).

Connected gadgets are already motivating us to change our habits to respect healthier lifestyles. They assist us in living fuller, longer lives by keeping our health and habits in check. The integration of technology in our everyday lives and education has altered the way we interact and communicate in society from basic skills such as the simple act of talking or choosing to send text messages over using the telephone. This has also had an influence on how or when we choose to take the time to communicate in person in order to reflect on and engage in meaningful conversation.

This mild social aversion can develop into an inhibition or reluctance to speak openly. And this trend has the potential to nudge its way into our classrooms (Ur, 1991), rendering social exchange, even in the context of an easy speaking activity, such as a simple ice-breaker exercise, a real issue. For any language teacher who is confronted with this type of problem in the early stages of their course syllabus, it can result in a really tedious and contagious challenge, as it can often spread from one student to another. An SCL environment can serve as a partial solution to this problem. As Jones (2007) points out, a student-centred approach encourages students to develop a 'can-do' attitude which is effective, motivating, and enjoyable for both the students and the teacher. In this way, the autonomous learning setting reinforces the notion of building strong foundations for a lifetime of learning.

In the context of English for academic purposes, Widdowson (1983, p. 41) argues that whether the language use is directly related to the specific disciplines that

Chapter 9

students are studying or not, it should make use of fundamental problem-solving methodology which is characteristic of academic study. Hence, an English course that is designed for students of Information and Communication (IC) studies should reflect the IC context in which various communication strategies are implemented to convey a specific message. The teaching of ESP should always reflect the underlying concepts and activities of the broader discipline (Dudley-Evans & St John, 1998). In addition, ESP teaching makes use of a methodology that differs from that used in general purpose English language teaching. Furthermore, Dudley-Evans and St John (1998) posit that the teacher can occasionally behave more like a language consultant, whilst enjoying equal status with the learners who have developed their own expertise in the subject matter. Consequently, as teaching and learning in higher education are part of a shared process (European Commission, 2013), the responsibility is subsequently both on the teacher *and* the student to contribute in order to achieve success. As we will see in this chapter, this shared process can additionally provide a flexible setting for the modification of teaching and learning roles. Inevitably, the use of technology both in the educational setting and outside the classroom, at home also has a fundamental role to play in preparing students for their future careers as professional candidates in the FIR.

1.2. An SCL approach to metacognitive skills development

If one of the fundamental objectives of education is to teach lifelong learning skills that will help people navigate through their careers and future relationships towards both personal and professional fulfilment, educators should then focus on teaching many soft skills, not only the hard skills, which refer to the core subjects that are more theoretical or knowledge-based in nature. Revered by 21st century professionals, these soft skills are characterised by the development of personal attributes (such as sociability, communicativeness, and thoughtfulness) that would enable someone to interact efficiently and harmoniously with other people, whether they be prospective clients or fellow colleagues. As Gray (2016) points out, soft skills as well as critical thinking skills and creativity will be much more valued in the professional workspace by the year 2020, whilst emotional intelligence and cognitive flexibility, which are not currently featured in the top ten today, will be added to the top skills needed list. The underlying foundation for acquiring these skills is an excellent combination of verbal and non-verbal communication skills, which make up a significant part of the essential soft skills. Transversal in nature and the basis for people skills or sociability, they are part of several competences and significant qualities to possess when considering positions that include negotiation, coordination, and management tasks. For this reason, language teachers should strive to assess both the current *and* future needs of students whilst including activities that place them at the heart of their own learning process. This will assist them in developing transversal metacognitive skills.

Consisting of both metacognitive knowledge and metacognitive experiences, metacognition is higher-order thinking which involves active control over the cognitive processes engaged in learning (Flavell, 1978). It plays a significant role in oral communication of information, persuasion, and comprehension, but also language acquisition, memory, problem-solving, social cognition and various types of self-control and self-instruction (Flavell, 1979). The integration of Flavell's (1978, 1979) theories in language lesson planning can prove to be beneficial for both the language learner and teacher who are in constant evolution, one in terms of learning and the other in terms of teaching. Mehisto, Marsh, and Frigols (2008) explain that thinking (cognition) is the mental faculty of knowing, which makes use of the following skills: perceiving, recognising, judging, reasoning, conceiving, and imagining. They express that cognition is a prerequisite in the engineering of lesson plans, however they also indicate that to heighten the intellectual challenge of a particular task for students, cognition must also be integrated into the task itself, so as to encourage the learners to engage and develop their own critical thinking and problem-solving abilities.

Within the framework of SCL, there is an emphasis on student involvement which fosters a classroom culture or mindset that aims at strengthening the learning process through the active participation of the student. As an innovative educational approach which has been shown to empower students, SCL encourages students to gain pragmatic knowledge whilst applying it to achieve specific goals and outcomes, as a European research project, the Peer Assessment of Student-Centred Learning (PASCL) explains (ESU, 2015). If learners are granted the authority and the freedom to create and make decisions, the process inevitably encourages them to ascertain and widen their creative potential, since they are in control of the various problem-solving stages whilst achieving specific learning outcomes. A recent study (Di Pardo Léon-Henri, 2015) has shown that these types of activities can also assist students in metacognitive skills development.

Whilst "governments are responsible for defining the policy, legal and funding contexts which impact on the motivation and ability of institutions to integrate new modes [of learning] across higher education provision[s]" (ESU, 2015, p. 35), the institutions themselves are responsible for the design of pedagogical approaches and curriculum that better correlate with the diverse needs and demands of today's students. This is the position of the High Level Group on the Modernisation of Higher Education of the European Commission (2013) which published a report entitled "The New Modes of teaching and learning in higher education" (p. 35). Moreover, as stated by ESU (2015), "the integration of digital technologies and pedagogies should form an integral element of higher education institutions' strategies for teaching and learning" (p. 35). In their report, the European Commission cites Allan Bloom, American philosopher, essayist, and academic, who critiques contemporary university in his book *The Closing of the American Mind*. Bloom (1987) maintains that the role of education in our times should ideally be to "find whatever there is in students that might yearn for completion and to reconstruct the learning that would enable them autonomously to seek that completion" (p. 63).

This is a founding principal of the SCL framework. Students feel empowered since there is a veritable shift in the classroom dynamic. The functioning of the classroom is flipped since the language teacher places the student at the centre of learning by responding to their needs. In assuming the role of moderator or facilitator, the teacher guides the student towards the defined objectives by favouring more autonomous learning strategies. Therefore, in this ESP setting, the traditional directive style of leading and teaching ('do as I say') is replaced by a more consultative approach. Composed of group work (two or more students), the syllabus in this setting involves clearly defined tasks, activities, and projects which promote learner autonomy in an SCL and ESP setting where students are encouraged to work towards improving and expanding their communication skills whilst exploring and developing learner strategies which can immediately be used to progress in their metacognitive development. Quite remarkably, much of this process is accomplished on a subconscious level and often it is in retrospect that the students are able to quantify and qualify how much they were able to accomplish together (Di Pardo Léon-Henri, 2015). These types of methods and procedures will ultimately serve them afterward in work-related settings (such as internships) and in due course, all throughout their professional career in the FIR.

As the PASCL project (ESU, 2015) demonstrates, students in an SCL setting are increasingly motivated because they are keenly implicated in sharing their knowledge and skills during the planning and implementation process. In addition, they are actively involved independent learners and decision-makers. If they are working within a team, they are also engrossed in the creativity, design, and decision-making process, which are activities that necessitate sharp communication and social skills. And yet, teaching these professional and metacognitive skills to learners requires that the educator must first deconstruct the components of an interaction and then develop an approach that can be implemented to encourage a variety of learners to manage diverse content under different time constraints whilst assisting the learner in developing metacognitive skills, such as self-reflection, in a secure, effective, and innovative learning environment.

2. Method

This qualitative content analysis study was conducted through classroom observation of an SCL environment in an ESP setting, the use of a questionnaire, and video sampling. The study took place over the course of two academic years (in 2016-2017 and 2017-2018) at the University of Franche-Comté. More specifically, it was introduced in the context of a mixed class of first year IC with

Chapter 9

language sciences students in the ESP Department of the University of Besançon (UFR SLHS). Both quantitative and qualitative research methods were used to analyse the survey results.

For the academic year 2016-2017, there were six classes composed of 123 students. The majority of the students (76% or 94 out of 123 students) were enrolled in IC studies. The language sciences students represented 24% (or 30 out of 123 students). During 2017-2018, there were approximately 140 students divided into five classes. The majority of the classes (74% or 104 out of 140 students) were composed of IC students, whilst language sciences students represented only 26% (or 36 out of 140 students) of the class. These statistics show that in terms of the number of students per domain, the two years are quite similar. In all, a total of 32 films were produced in this study for the academic year 2016-2017 and 35 films were produced for 2017-2018.

2.1. Setting and procedure

At the outset of their three-year Bachelor's programme, students must possess many different professional, interpersonal, and domain specific skills. For instance, they must be at ease with the use of modern modes of communication (from business software to various types of technology). They are required to not only work efficiently and independently, but at the same time they must be capable of using their soft skills to communicate within a culturally diverse team. The development of metacognitive and verbal as well as non-verbal communication skills is also required so as to facilitate professional interaction in particularly challenging situations, such as negotiation. And finally, they must acquire strong written, oral, and professional skills in English.

The project was given to the students during the second half of their first year of studies. On the first day of class, the students were encouraged to reflect on their verbal and non-verbal communication skills in order to go beyond their words and actions with the objective of motivating and inspiring others, but also arousing emotion and awareness on the topic of their choice. Since each class was composed of approximately 30 students from two different yet similar domains, the majority of the students did not know each other at the onset. This setting served as a real opportunity since all of the students faced the same social challenge of having to overcome fears whilst taking the risks associated with meeting new people.

After a few quick ice-breaker exercises, based on the notion of verbal and non-verbal communication, the students formed their groups of four, five, or six individuals, at the most. They were then invited to watch, analyse, and critique two award-winning videos entitled *Colors 2015* (Harikrishnan, 2015) and *The Wall 2016* (Naderi, 2016). After a few viewings, the students were asked to first consider the message, then the direction, and all aspects and qualities relating to the films. Many of the group members were in possession of tablets, laptops or smartphones, and they were invited to review the film as many times as they wished. After preparing a summary of their observations (which was collected as an initial written evaluation), each group briefly presented their observations. An open discussion and informal debate on the effectiveness of film techniques (such as the choice of verbal or non-verbal communication, the absence or use of emotional music) ensued.

The five year running Toronto Short Film Festival (http://www.torontoshort.com/), which in fact served as the inspiration for this pedagogical approach, was also explained to the students. And finally, the One-Minute Film Project, which would be spread over the course of the semester in the form of different tasks and workshops, was fully presented to the students. All of the above was done during the first class of the semester, which was composed of twelve two-hour sessions.

2.2. The One-Minute Film Project: make a message that counts

Simply stated, the students were asked to produce a one-minute film with a poignant message. Even though the students in these domains are not film students per se, they are part of a very visually inclined generation which loves to use technology, photographs or film, and to be photographed and filmed. In this SCL setting, the students were given *carte blanche* and the freedom to choose any theme they wanted. In addition, they were encouraged to use a variety of film techniques. They could choose to use verbal or non-verbal communication or a combination of both. Deadlines were rapidly set for the scenario (which needed to be approved by the teacher in the second week) and dialogue submission (a few weeks later). The evaluation grid[3] and links to additional films (this should include many different styles from the first historical films, such as Charlie Chaplin style or modern day creations) were made available on Moodle with the course syllabus, so that students could find inspiration and be creative. Since the students were encouraged to meet often outside the classroom, to prepare, rehearse, and shoot their film, this project needed to be presented very early on in the semester.

During the semester, the teacher provided an introductory course on several communication and linguistic subjects, such as: verbal and non-verbal cues, intercultural communication, cultural *faux pas*, English language history, linguistics, and sociolinguistics, as well as dialects and the psychology of dialects. Many of the associated exercises involved the observation, analysis, and critique of oral presentation skills and particularly the role and impact of body language (in advertisements for example) and the importance of voice projection. This often led to self-reflection on ways to learn new strategies in order to improve these communication skills.

As we have seen, within the framework of SCL, students gain pragmatic knowledge whilst applying it to achieve specific goals and outcomes. When they are granted the authority and the freedom to create and make decisions during the creative process, they have the freedom to make decisions based on the various problem-solving stages. For this reason, the teacher only intervened during the initial film validation process and scenario approval early on in the semester. Then, two one-hour in-class workshops were scheduled (at Week 2 and Week 6) for the students to independently plan and work on the project, whilst solving and exchanging their ideas in their film groups. During these workshops, the teacher was available to guide the students in their research and review their communication strategies. The role of the teacher was to mediate and facilitate

---

3. Refer to supplementary materials, Appendix 2 "Evaluation Criteria and Scoring for One-Minute Short Films".

by only answering questions, if necessary. One of the most important points here is for the teacher to adopt a passive approach and avoid influencing or inhibiting the student's creativity flow.

The films were then sent to the teacher (via We Transfer) before Week 9, so that a film viewing workshop could be organised for Week 10. During this workshop, the students were able to view their films and analyse the techniques and messages, as well as the reactions of their classmates. The observation of this exercise was also a significant moment for the teacher in terms of research since the feedback was not only verbal but also non-verbal. It was clearly stated that the spoken critiques needed to be tactful, supportive, and of a creative nature. In their groups, the students were asked for written feedback. They had to decipher the main message and provide their honest feelings for the teacher to read. They were given the freedom to explicitly express their opinions, by writing down their thoughts, perhaps by sharing something they would not have said in open class discussion.

3. Results and discussion

This study ultimately serves to determine if it is possible to adopt an innovative student-centred pedagogical approach that combines new technologies with teaching methods that stimulate student motivation, whilst encouraging the development of professional and metacognitive skills within the context of non-specialist English language students. At the same time, the study investigates the students' impressions on the pedagogical intervention through the use of a questionnaire[4]. This questionnaire was originally conceived and created by closely examining and decomposing the various stages and activities involved in preparing the final one-minute film task.

For the year 2016-2017, n=114 students out of a total of 123 students responded to the questionnaire online. A swift analysis of the responses reveals that the vast majority 78% (or 89 out of 114 students) strongly agreed or somewhat agreed

---

4. The survey (see supplementary materials, Appendix 3: "One-Minute Film Project Questionnaire") was uploaded to Google Drive.

(37 of the 123 students or 33%) with the statement that all of the group members worked actively together on the scenario. The results were similar when asked about the realisation phase. A total of n=45 students (or 40%) strongly agreed that all of the group members worked actively together on the filmmaking process, whilst n=44 students (or 39%) somewhat agreed. The number of students who indicated that they strongly agreed and enjoyed working on a group project was n=48 (or 42%) and n=41 students (or 36%) somewhat agreed. A total of n=11 (or 9% of the) students expressed that they did not like working in groups for reasons related to scheduling problems, differences of opinions, and lack of motivation on behalf of some of the group members. However, at the same time n=64 students (or 56%) strongly agreed that working in groups (peer collaborative work) is an effective way to learn language/communication skills. Furthermore, in terms of metacognitive skills development, n=53 students (or 47%) strongly agreed that this project encourages creativity, critical thinking, and the development of collaboration skills, whilst n=46 students (or 41%) somewhat agree with this statement. When asked if this project is more challenging and interesting than the traditional oral presentation, the vast majority, n=65 students (or 57%), expressed that they strongly agree and n=30 students (or 26%) somewhat agreed. N=59 students (or 52%) strongly agreed that an active approach or learning by doing is the best method for learning, whilst n=34 (or 30%) somewhat agreed on this point. A very large majority, n=88 students (or 77%) strongly agreed that the One-Minute Film Project should become an annual contest open to all university students at the UFR SLHS, whilst only n=23 students (or 20%) disagreed. Concerning the recurrent themes chosen by the students, they were mainly based on topics which are central to the lives of undergraduates, for instance: peer pressure, alcoholism, homelessness, xenophobia, intercultural awareness, technology abuse, and harassment.

A preliminary analysis of the results has shown that this pedagogical intervention provides many beneficial outcomes associated with an SCL environment. The rationale behind choosing the film as the medium is that although role play lies at the heart of this project, the small groups of students must define and deconstruct the messages they are striving to communicate in their film. In this way, the students are placed at the centre of their learning whilst using a medium that clearly appeals to them, as the survey results have shown. Whilst being empowered with the ability to create something that does not exist, they are fully in control of the steps and stages of the project. The teacher adopts a secondary role of consultant and simply accompanies them throughout the stages. In the end, all of the decision-making process is shared and negotiated by the team, which must consider and respect the various needs and demands of their individual team members. Problem-solving, for example, on topics such as how to shoot and edit a film on a smartphone requires a group effort and, in some cases, additional independent research. As challenging as it maybe, the teacher does not provide all of the answers to their questions and in this particular case, merely encourages the students to adopt a more curious or autonomous stance and actively search for tutorials online. The scenario, dialogue, spoken critiques, and written feedback all serve as evaluators and indicators of linguistic competency in terms of formative and summative assessment. All of the different collaborative stages encourage discussion, debate, and conversations, as well as proofreading to ensure that the grammatical errors and spelling mistakes are kept to a minimum. The ultimate objective of the approach is to encourage soft skills development and better equip students who must face competitive technophile candidates in a job market which has substantially been modified and transformed by artificial intelligence during the FIR.

4. Conclusion and future directions

It is our position that exploring this type of pedagogical approach which could be adapted to suit any language class (within an ESP context or not), will assist students in improving their soft skills and preparing for the job market in a highly competitive FIR. In addition, it could also serve as the basis of a future transversal study, which could include specialists in sociology and psychology to lead a more in depth analysis of the chosen themes, the intentions behind those themes, and the ways in which the students choose to construct and weave their message into their films. Furthermore, the integration of artificial intelligence use (in the form of robotics, for example) in the course syllabus at the higher education level could prove to be instructive and revealing for both the students and the researching educator, thus contributing new insights for our field of study.

And finally, there is increasing interest in using this type of short film and photography as a form of expression since the European Commission (https://europa.eu/euandme/en/yfc/) has also announced a young filmmaker's competition entitled #EUandME. Perhaps the ultimate objective of this film project could be to submit a few of the best films to this type of competition, with the approval of the directors, authors, and actors, of course.

Acknowledgements

I would like to thank all of the students who participated in this two-year study for their creativity, personal investment, and high level of motivation. These poignant films are a reflection of who you are, what you believe, and what is happening in your world. Even during this small-scale study, you have taken many risks and produced a lasting universal message in the form of film. You have successfully gone way beyond your words and actions.

Supplementary materials

https://research-publishing.box.com/s/ba0z0ihs0ihazy0xgr9mqk5sykt6qq3s

References

Bloom, A. (1987). *The closing of the American mind: how higher education has failed democracy and impoverished the souls of today's students.* Simon & Schuster.

Di Pardo Léon-Henri, D. (2015). CLIL in the business english classroom: from language learning to the development of professional communication and metacognitive skills. *ELTWorldOnline, April, Special Issue on CLIL.* https://blog.nus.edu.sg/eltwo/files/2015/04/CLIL-in-the-Business-English-Classroom_editforpdf-2da6nlw.pdf

Dudley-Evans, T., & St John, M. J. (1998). *Developments in English for specific purposes.* Cambridge University Press.

ESU. (2015). *Overview on student-centred learning in higher education: research study.* European Students' Union. https://www.esu-online.org/wp-content/uploads/2016/07/Overview-on-Student-Centred-Learning-in-Higher-Education-in-Europe.pdf

European Commission. (2013). *High level group on the modernisation of higher education. Report to the European Commission on improving the quality of teaching and learning in Europe's higher education institutions.* Publications Office of the European Union. https://publications.europa.eu/en/publication-detail/-/publication/fbd4c2aa-aeb7-41ac-ab4c-a94feea9eb1f

Flavell, J. H. (1978, August). Metacognition. In E. Langer (Chair), *Current perspectives on awareness and cognitive processes.* Symposium presented at the meeting of the American Psychological Association, Toronto, Canada.

Flavell, J. H. (1979). Metacognition and cognitive monitoring: a new area of cognitive developmental inquiry. *American Psychologist, 34*(10), 906-911. https://doi.org/10.1037/0003-066x.34.10.906

Gray, A. (2016, Jan 19). The 10 skills you need to thrive in the fourth industrial revolution. *World Economic Forum.* https://www.weforum.org/agenda/2016/01/the-10-skills-you-need-to-thrive-in-the-fourth-industrial-revolution/

Harikrishnan, G. (2015). *Colors* [Yatna Films, India]. https://www.youtube.com/watch?v=D2MJh5Av16w

Jones, L. (2007). *The student-centred classroom.* Cambridge University Press.

Mehisto, P., Marsh, D., & Frigols, M.-J. (2008). *Uncovering CLIL: content and language integrated learning in bilingual and multilingual education.* Macmillan Publishing.

Naderi, F. (2016). *The Wall* [Sanandaj, Iran]. http://www.torontourbanfilmfestival.com/films/wall-1

Schwab, K. (2016, Jan 14). The fourth industrial revolution: what it means, how to respond. *World Economic Forum.* https://www.weforum.org/agenda/2016/01/the-fourth-industrial-revolution-what-it-means-and-how-to-respond/

Ur, P. (1991). *A course in language. Teaching: practice and theory.* Cambridge University Press.

Widdowson, H. G. (1983). Learning purpose and language use. Oxford University Press.

10. Pronunciation instruction in ESP teaching to enhance students' prosody

Leticia Quesada Vázquez[1]

Abstract

This study investigates the efficacy of explicit rhythm instruction to improve engineering students' prosody in English. A pronunciation module of ten weekly sessions of 30 minutes held within the class schedule was designed for a technical English course at Rovira i Virgili University. Sessions were outlined using a communicative framework. Two hundred and ninety eight Spanish/Catalan students were divided into three experimental groups receiving rhythm instruction, and three control groups which did not. Students were recorded before and after the training. Six native American English speakers were also recorded as a reference point. VarcoV values were measured and compared using PRAAT and the data were analysed using mixed analysis of variances (ANOVAS) and t-tests. Results reveal that the experimental group tends to increase in VarcoV after training, approaching English rhythm, while the control group presents incongruences. Despite results not always being significant, an analysis of the effect sizes for the t-tests comparing before and after VarcoV values for the experimental vs. the control groups shows significance. These results support the hypothesis that rhythm instruction can be beneficial to improve English for Specific Purposes (ESP) students' prosody.

Keywords: ESP, rhythm instruction, VarcoV.

---

1. Rovira i Virgili University, Tarragona, Spain; leticia.quesada@urv.cat; https://orcid.org/0000-0002-7422-6251

How to cite this chapter: Quesada Vázquez, L. (2019). Pronunciation instruction in ESP teaching to enhance students' prosody. In S. Papadima-Sophocleous, E. Kakoulli Constantinou & C. N. Giannikas (Eds), *ESP teaching and teacher education: current theories and practices* (pp. 163-176). Research-publishing.net. https://doi.org/10.14705/rpnet.2019.33.932

Chapter 10

1. Introduction

Effective communication has always been at the core of ESP teaching (Dudley-Evans & St John, 1998). Since its inception in the 1960s, ESP has aimed at meeting students' needs for competent communication in their professional environments, especially of those tertiary learners who live and study in non-English speaking countries (Tzoannopoulou, 2015). Moreover, the launching of the Bologna Process in European universities has fostered the need for more ESP courses which advocate for enhancing communicative skills that favour the international market and the mobility derived from it (Räisänen & Fortanet-Gómez, 2008; Wilkinson, 2008).

It has been observed that ESP students may have the knowledge to face a communicative situation but, according to Douglas (2000), they often fail to effectively transmit and interact in the target language. Walker and White (2013) argue that, in contexts where learners have to speak, the practice of language skills that ensure communication can reduce students' anxiety and improve their intelligibility and fluency. Active listening, questioning, spoken interaction, and oral presentation rehearsal are some of the tools recommended so as to achieve this purpose (Dudley-Evans & St John, 1998). Nevertheless, not much attention has been paid to the application of these tools and others to pronunciation teaching in order to improve ESP students' intelligibility, comprehensibility, and fluency.

Pronunciation has often been neglected within English as a Second Language (ESL) and English as a Foreign Language (EFL) classrooms for several reasons, such as lack of time, teachers' limited training, or insufficient guarantee of lasting results (Derwing & Munro, 2015). Besides, the dichotomy between the nativeness and intelligibility principles (Levis, 2005) directly affects pronunciation teaching. Pronunciation instruction has long been associated with an ideal of nativeness, i.e. achieving a fully L1 English speaker accent. Consequently, the more native-like an ESL learner sounds when speaking English, the better he/she will be understood. However, such an ambitious goal is rarely achieved and students can become highly demotivated in their way to succeed. This frustrating attempt to reach the perfect pronunciation is more evident in adults, who have passed the critical period and may suffer from fossilisation (Levis, 2005). As for ESP students for whom English becomes just another working tool, sounding like a native speaker does not tend to be an appealing aim to achieve, but they would rather work at being understandable when communicating in the target language. Hence, the intelligibility principle, which claims to focus on just the aspects that guarantee communication and comprehension, seems to adjust better to ESP students' expectations. Nevertheless, determining which pronunciation features are more useful to teach for communicative purposes is not always an easy task and requires a deep analysis of the students' needs.

Experts agree that suprasegmental features play a more important role in global prosody than segmental ones. Suprasegmentals help the speech sound coherent and connect concepts that go beyond the meaning of isolated words (Gilbert, 2008). However, time is always tight in the ESL classroom, since several skills have to be taught. Therefore, deciding which is the feature that best meets the needs of each particular group of students becomes essential to ensure the proper functioning of the classroom (Basturkmen, 2010). ESP students are not language-oriented, so it is better to opt for simple and practical features that are easy to understand. Besides, their main aim is to be able to communicate, so fluency and comprehensibility issues are key in their learning process. Some studies have proved, by manipulating second language learners' speeches artificially, that the more L2-like the rhythm of their speech is, the more intelligible the speech becomes (Quene & Van Delf, 2010; Tajima, Port, & Dalby, 1997). As a consequence, language rhythm postulates as a plausible candidate.

Rhythm is found in the foundations of speech, organising thoughts, and connecting ideas. When the rhythm of a language is modified, the speech does not meet the listeners' expectations: it does not anticipate the lexical and syntactic information needed for an effective comprehension of the message (Derwing & Munro, 2015). Hence, both production and perception become compromised and misunderstandings and communication breakdowns arise. When speaking a second language, students tend to adopt their mother tongue rhythm, since they are not aware of the differences in rhythm among languages.

Consequently, students alter the rhythm of the target language, making the speech difficult to follow. Syllable-timed languages, on the one hand, and stress-timed languages, on the other hand, are placed at the extremes of the rhythm continuum: Spanish and Catalan are syllable-timed languages, so their rhythm is based on syllables that have approximately the same duration when pronounced. Lloyd James (1940) compared Spanish to a machine gun shot. English, however, is a stress-timed language, basing its rhythm on two different beats defined by stress: stressed syllables, which are pronounced longer, and unstressed syllables, which are pronounced shorter. In this case, Lloyd James related it to a morse code message. For this reason, Spanish and Catalan students are often said to sound chopped and pause wrongly when speaking English, a fact that negatively affects their fluency and comprehensibility in the second language.

Several studies have proved that the introduction of rhythmic cues in the EFL classroom can improve learners' intelligibility, fluency, and comprehensibility (Chela-Flores, 1997; Hahn, 2004; Tsiartsioni, 2011). Chela-Flores (1997) designed word-decontextualised patterns to be taught to Spanish students at the university of Zulia, in Venezuela, for a semester. Results revealed that students improved in both perception and recognition under controlled circumstances. Hahn (2004) investigated primary stress with international teaching assistants in the US. Three different versions of the same speech were created based on primary stress: a version where primary stress was correctly placed, a second one where it was incorrectly placed, and a third one where it was missing. American university students assessed the intelligibility of the speeches and results showed that the version where primary stress was correctly placed was considered more intelligible. Tsiartsioni (2011) worked with three age groups of EFL Greek students (6, 12, and 16 years old). Each age group was further divided into an experimental group that received rhythm instruction and a control group that did not. When calculating vocalic and consonantal Pairwise Variability Indexes (vocPVI and consPVI, respectively), it was observed that the experimental group improved its rhythm while the control group failed to do so. Little research on rhythm instruction has been conducted with ESP students. Chela-Flores (1993) introduced rhythm training within an ESP reading course in a nonnative environment obtaining encouraging results on listening discrimination (as cited in Chela-Flores, 1993). The current study investigates the effectiveness of rhythm instruction within an ESP course to improve the students' prosody in the target language. For this purpose, the following hypotheses have been formulated:

- the introduction of a pronunciation module based on Celce-Murcia, Brinton, and Goodwin's (1996) steps to teach communicatively will help students improve their L2 global prosody;

- students' L1 *negative transfer* (Celce-Murcia et al., 1996, p. 20) will decrease more when receiving explicit rhythm instruction; and

- students' rhythm will approach more that of L1 English speakers' when receiving explicit rhythm instruction.

2. Method

The present study is associated with an extended project that focusses on the effectiveness of explicit rhythm instruction within the EFL classroom. For this purpose, a classroom-based pronunciation research study (Derwing & Munro, 2015) was conducted. This empirical longitudinal study examined the progress of first-year undergraduate engineering students attending a compulsory B2 technical English course, which took place from February to May 2017 at Rovira i Virgili University. A pronunciation module was designed and embedded as part of the course. It consisted of thirty-minute sessions taught for ten weeks within regular classes. Two hundred and ninety-eight students were randomly divided into three experimental groups which received rhythm instruction during the sessions, and three control groups which did not. All the students were recorded before (pre-test) and after (post-test) training. The test consisted of four exercises: reading ten sentences and a text aloud, introducing themselves, and giving their opinion on social media. They were recorded individually in three isolated rooms at the university library using two Sony PCM-M1O and a Zoom H4nsp recorders. Besides, six native American English speaking visiting students from Bates College, (Maine, USA), were also recorded taking the test as a reference point.

This study concentrates on the acoustic analysis of the rhythm of the sentences uttered by those students who completed the treatment, and compares them with those of the natives. For this purpose, VarcoV values were measured. VarcoV is a rhythmic measure that estimates "the standard deviation of vocalic interval duration divided by mean vocalic duration, multiplied by 100" (White & Mattys, 2007, p. 508). After comparing several rhythmic measures, White and Mattys (2007) concluded that VarcoV was the most reliable measure in order to assess rhythm within the second language field. Due to its wider variation in syllable length, English shows higher VarcoV values than Spanish/Catalan. Hence, this study aims to examine, on the one hand, if ESP students' values increase after treatment and if there is a difference in results depending on the instruction received and, on the other hand, how the results obtained approach natives' values. The values of each of the sentences were obtained using PRAAT (www.praat.org). The boundaries of vocalic and consonant interval clusters were marked for each sentence, and Ordin and Polyanskaya's (2014, 2015) script[2] was run. Pauses were not considered in the analysis.

The data were analysed statistically with mixed repeated measures ANOVAS and t-tests. First of all, the effect of each instruction was examined by carrying out a mixed ANOVA with time (before and after instruction) and sentence as within-subjects factors, group (experimental or control) as a between-subjects factor, and VarcoV values as the dependent variable. Then, we were interested in studying the degree of variation between utterances before and after treatment for each group. Hence, a second mixed ANOVA was performed, this time with the difference in VarcoV values between the sentences before and after training as the dependent variable, sentence as the within-subjects factor and group as the between-subjects factor. Next, four t-tests were run for each sentence in order to analyse the impact of the difference depending on the instruction received: two paired-samples t-tests that compared the groups' learning process, and two-

---

2. The VarcoV values obtained from Ordin and Polyanskaya's (2014, 2015) script do not include the multiplication by 100, unlike specified in White and Mattys (2007).

independent-samples t-tests comparing the initial and final performance of the two groups. Finally, the effect sizes of the difference between sentences before and after instruction were further studied by performing one more independent-samples t-test. For all the tests, the alpha value was always set at .05[3].

2.1. Participants

Only the students who attended 90% of the sessions were considered to have fulfilled the treatment. Unfortunately, a lot of them dropped out or skipped sessions, so they had to be dismissed. In the end, 42 students could be used as subjects, 21 per group. The profile of these students was quite homogeneous: they were all between 18 and 20 years old, mostly balanced bilinguals of Spanish and Catalan; there were two students who were dominant in Spanish and three students whose mother tongue was a different language. However, all of them pursued primary and secondary education in Catalonia and, consequently, their command of both languages was high. The main difference between students was their initial level of English: the control group started with a slightly higher level of English (four low-intermediate, eleven intermediate, and six advanced students) than the experimental group (ten low-intermediate, six intermediate, and five advanced students). However, this variability had already been predicted because of the different educational backgrounds of ESP students (some of them coming from high school, others from vocational training), so level was not considered a determinant factor affecting the outcome of the treatment.

2.2. The pronunciation module

Sessions followed Celce-Murcia et al.'s (1996) steps to teach communicatively so as to guarantee a communicative framework. They all started with a description and analysis of the aspect to be taught. Next, students listened to some podcasts in order to distinguish and get familiar with the feature. Finally, they practised the item at three different levels: controlled practice, doing activities like reading aloud, and *listen and repeat*; guided practice, playing

---
3. Statistics have been verified by Prof. Urbano Lorenzo, Rovira i Virgili University.

guessing games, and doing gap-filling exercises; and communicative practice by participating in group discussions and debates.

The module was scheduled according to the syllabus of the course, i.e. the grammar and vocabulary used had already been taught in class. This way, students could concentrate better on practising their speaking skills and, at the same time, their motivation was guaranteed because they continued working on concepts directly related to their disciplines (Anderson-Hsieh, 1990). Regarding materials, activities were adapted from several pronunciation books and research papers by mainly modifying rhythm activities to use technical vocabulary, or they were created from scratch by using online resources such as videos or images.

3. Results and discussion

VarcoV means were calculated for each of the sentences. Table 1 compiles the means and standard deviations obtained for the experimental and the control group, both before and after treatment, and for the natives.

Table 1. VarcoV means per sentence

Group	Sentence				
	1	2	3	4	5
Control pre-test	0.37 (0.08)	0.40 (0.09)	0.39 (0.12)	0.54 (0.09)	0.45 (0.09)
Control post-test	0.36 (0.11)	0.40 (0.09)	0.38 (0.10)	0.52 (0.08)	0.47 (0.14)
Experimental pre-test	0.39 (0.11)	0.38 (0.07)	0.38 (0.10)	0.50 (0.09)	0.41 (0.09)
Experimental post-test	0.40 (0.08)	0.39 (0.08)	0.39 (0.13)	0.51 (0.09)	0.50 (0.12)
Natives	**0.33* (0.08)**	**0.48 (0.03)**	**0.36* (0.06)**	**0.56 (0.07)**	**0.57 (0.06)**
Group	Sentence				
	6	7	8	9	10
Control pre-test	0.48 (0.12)	0.55 (0.10)	0.42 (0.07)	0.49 (0.10)	0.48 (0.11)

Control post-test	0.49 (0.10)	0.53 (0.09)	0.43 (0.08)	0.51 (0.13)	0.52 (0.11)
Experimental pre-test	0.45 (0.10)	0.53 (0.13)	0.41 (0.08)	0.52 (0.11)	0.48 (0.05)
Experimental post-test	0.45 (0.09)	0.56 (0.09)	0.43 (0.06)	0.48 (0.09)	0.51 (0.08)
Natives	**0.53 (0.06)**	**0.64 (0.05)**	**0.50 (0.05)**	**0.47* (0.07)**	**0.52 (0.11)**

By examining the means, several observations could be made. Firstly, as expected, VarcoV values were generally higher for native speakers than for second language learners. There were three exceptions, though: Sentences 1, 3, and 9 (marked with an asterisk). In these cases, natives' values were noticeably lower than those of the ESP students. By examining the sentences in depth (see supplementary materials), it could be observed that Sentences 1 and 3 were much shorter than the rest. Natives tended to speak more slowly in these sentences, vocalizing excessively, and even pausing in unnatural places, showing an intentional will to sound clear. They seemed to be more aware of the need to make themselves understood. On the other hand, they uttered longer sentences in a more natural way, maintaining a more constant rhythm. This phenomenon could explain why natives' VarcoV values are lower in these sentences. However, Sentence 9 was not short and showed lower VarcoV values too. ESP students struggled a lot when reading this sentence, leading to many mispronunciations, a fact that could have affected results. However, further research should be conducted to prove this point.

Secondly, the experimental group tended to increase its VarcoV values after treatment, approaching native performance, while the control group behaved incongruently. Shadowed in grey, the increase in VarcoV for the experimental group was discernible in eight out of the ten sentences while the control group's figures only rose in half of them. Thus, numbers suggested that explicit rhythm instruction helped students to adopt the rhythm of the target language. It is true that the control group showed higher values in some of the sentences, closer to native figures. However, control group students started with a higher initial English level, so higher values were expected regardless of instruction.

Chapter 10

As previously mentioned, in order to determine the significance of the effect of the instruction, a mixed repeated measures ANOVA was carried out with time and sentence as within-subjects factors and group as a between-subjects factor. Non-significant results were found for both time $F(1,40)=2.006$, $p=.164$, and group $F(1,40)=.267$, $p=.608$, but they were significant in regards to sentence, $F(9,32)=29.172$, $p=.01$. However, the time*sentence interaction did not show significance, $F(9,32) = 1.185$, $p =.313$. Despite a lack of statistical significance, a clear impact of explicit rhythm instruction could be observed in Figure 1.

Figure 1. VarcoV progress after instruction

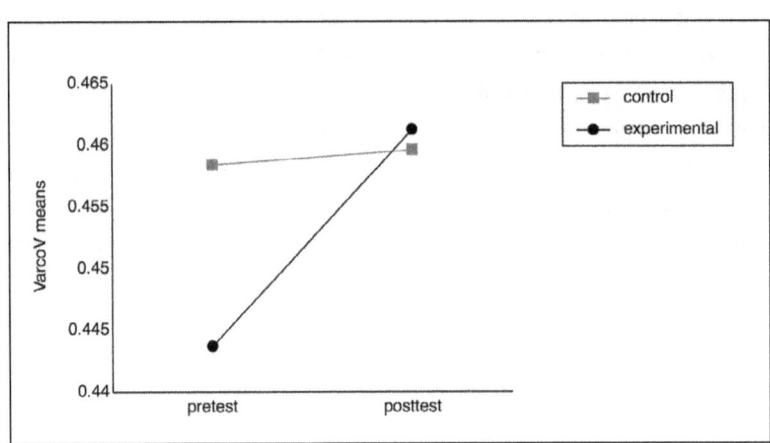

While the control group remained almost stable after treatment, the experimental group underwent a sharp increase after instruction. Hence, a positive effect of explicit rhythm instruction was still detected.

So as to examine the disparity in figures before and after treatment based on the instruction received, the second mixed ANOVA was run. The differences in VarcoV values before and after training were the dependent variable, sentence was the within-subjects factor, and group was the between-subjects factor. No significance was shown for either group, $F(1,40)=1.532$, $p=.223$, or sentence, $F(9,32)=1.185$, $p=.313$. The sentence*group interaction was also non-significant $F(9,32)=.961$, $p=.456$.

T-tests were further performed to look for variations within each sentence. For each sentence, four different t-tests were performed: two paired-samples t-tests comparing each group and two independent-samples t-tests comparing both groups before and after instruction. Neither the t-tests ($p>.05$) nor the corresponding effect sizes ($d<2$) showed significance. Nevertheless, a difference between the experimental and the control group effect sizes was observed when analysing paired-samples t-tests for each of the sentences. While the experimental group tended to display a positive difference, the control group shows more negative ones and, when the difference was positive, it was still smaller than for the experimental one (Table 2).

Table 2. Effect sizes of control and experimental paired-sample t-tests per sentence

Effect sizes difference per sentence										
Group	Sentence									
	1	2	3	4	5	6	7	8	9	10
Control	-1.28	0.06	-0.12	-0.23	0.13	0.04	-1.73	0.12	0.11	0.31
Experimental	1.77	0.08	0.06	0.17	0.65	-0.05	0.24	0.25	-0.26	0.39

For this reason, another independent-sample t-test was performed to analyse the relevance of the effect size. This time, results were statistically significant $T(18)=-2102$, $p=.05$. Findings revealed a better performance when teaching rhythm explicitly. Nevertheless, further research needs to be conducted to reach more conclusive results.

4. Conclusions

By comparing students' progress after pronunciation instruction and correlating it to the native speaker counterparts, this study examines the effectiveness of specific pronunciation teaching (in this case, explicit rhythm instruction) on ESP students' prosody. Several limitations such as a dramatic decrease of the population under study, overcrowded classes, or limited time for instruction should be taken into account when interpreting the statistical non-significance of the results. Still, explicit rhythm instruction is shown to increase students' VarcoV values in most of the sentences analysed, enhancing students' acquisition of the rhythm of the target language, and consequently decreasing the negative transfer from their mother tongue. Besides, figures tend to get closer to the native equivalents. On the contrary, a lack of this kind of training results in inconsistent behaviour. Findings, hence, suggest that ESP students' prosody can improve by means of explicit rhythm instruction, but more research has to be conducted in order to reach statistical significance. On the other hand, as the control group also shows signs of improvement in some sentences, pronunciation seems to arise as a beneficial aspect to teach within the ESP classroom.

Acknowledgements

This research was funded by a Martí i Franquès doctoral grant from Universitat Rovira i Virgili and the project FFI2017-84479-P from the Spanish Ministry of Economy and Business.

Supplementary materials

https://research-publishing.box.com/s/kqyiwxmatusypidyrfawezo6uw3z1zl3

References

Anderson-Hsieh, J. (1990). Teaching suprasegmentals to international teaching assistants using field-specific materials. *English for Specific Purposes, 9*(3), 195-214. https://doi.org/10.1016/0889-4906(90)90013-3

Basturkmen, H. (2010). *Developing courses in English for specific purposes*. Palgrave Macmillan.

Celce-Murcia, M., Brinton, D. M., & Goodwin, J. M. (1996). *Teaching pronunciation: a reference for teachers of English to speakers of other languages*. Cambridge University Press.

Chela-Flores, B. (1993). On the acquisition of English rhythm: theoretical and practice issues. *Lenguas Modernas, 20*, 151-164.

Chela-Flores, B. (1997). Rhythmic patterns as basic units in pronunciation teaching. *Onomázein, 2*, 111-134. http://onomazein.letras.uc.cl/Articulos/2/4_Chela.pdf

Derwing, T. M., & Munro, M. J. (2015). *Pronunciation fundamentals. Evidence-based perspectives for L2 teaching and research*. John Benjamins.

Douglas, D. (2000). *Assessing language for specific purposes*. Cambridge University Press.

Dudley-Evans, T., & St John, M. (1998). *Developments in English for specific purposes: a multidisciplinary approach*. Cambridge University Press.

Gilbert, J. B. (2008). *Teaching pronunciation: using the prosody pyramid*. Cambridge University Press.

Hahn, L. (2004). Primary stress and intelligibility: research to motivate the teaching of suprasegmentals. *TESOL Quarterly, 38*(2) 201-223. https://doi.org/10.2307/3588378

Levis, J. M. (2005). Changing contexts and shifting paradigms in pronunciation teaching. *TESOL Quarterly, 39*(3) 369-378. https://doi.org/10.2307/3588485

Lloyd James, A. (1940). *Speech signals in telephony*. Pitman & Sons.

Ordin, M., & Polyanskaya, L. (2014). Development of timing patterns in first and second languages. *System, 42*, 244-257. https://doi.org/10.1016/j.system.2013.12.004

Ordin, M., & Polyanskaya, L. (2015). Acquisition of speech rhythm in a second language by learners with rhythmically different native languages. *The Journal of the Acoustical Society of America, 138*(2), 533-544. https://doi.org/10.1121/1.4923359

Quene, H., & Van Delft, L. E. (2010). Non-native durational patterns decrease speech intelligibility. *Speech Communication, 52*(11-12), 911-918. https://doi.org/10.1016/j.specom.2010.03.005

Räisänen, C., & Fortanet-Gómez, I. (2008). The state of ESP teaching and learning in Western European higher education after Bologna. In I. Fortanet-Gómez & C. Räisänen (Eds), *ESP in European higher education. Integrating language and content* (pp. 11-51). John Benjamins. https://doi.org/10.1075/aals.4.03rai

Tajima, K., Port, R., & Dalby, J. (1997). The effects of temporal correction on intelligibility of foreign-accented English. *Journal of Phonetics, 25*(1), 1-24. https://doi.org/10.1006/jpho.1996.0031

Tsiartsioni, E. (2011). Can pronunciation be taught? Teaching English speech rhythm to Greek students. In E. Kitis, N. Lavidas, N. Tpointzi & T. Tsangalidis (Eds), *Selected papers from the 19th International Symposium on Theoretical and Applied Linguistics (ISTAL 19) (pp. 447-458)*. Aristotle University of Thessaloniki.

Tzoannopoulou, M. (2015). Rethinking ESP: integrating content and language in the university classroom. *Procedia - Social and Behavioral Sciences, 173*, 149-153. https://doi.org/10.1016/j.sbspro.2015.02.045

Walker, A., & White, G. (2013). *Technology enhanced language teaching: connecting theory and practice.* Oxford University Press.

White, L., & Mattys, S. (2007). Calibrating rhythm: first language and second language studies. *Journal of Phonetics, 35*(4), 501-522. https://doi.org/10.1016/j.wocn.2007.02.003

Wilkinson, R. (2008). Locating the ESP space in problem-based learning: English-medium degree programmes from a post-Bologna perspective. In I. Fortanet-Gómez & C. A. Räisänen (Eds), *ESP in European Higher Education: Integrating Language and Content* (pp. 55-73). John Benjamins. https://doi.org/10.1075/aals.4.05wil

Author index

A
Aleksić-Hajduković, Irena 4, 47

B
Bullock, Neil 5, 79

D
Di Pardo Léon-Henri, Dana 7, 147

G
Giannikas, Christina Nicole 1, 5, 11, 95

K
Kakoulli Constantinou, Elis 1, 3, 11, 27
Kırkgöz, Yasemin 3, 13

M
Mijomanović, Stevan 4, 47

N
Nikiforou, Eleni 6, 131

P
Papadima-Sophocleous, Salomi 1, 3, 6, 10, 27, 111
Pappa, Giouli 6, 111

Q
Quesada Vázquez, Leticia 7, 163

S
Sinadinović, Danka 4, 47
Souleles, Nicos 3, 27

Z
Zareva, Alla 4, 63

www.ingramcontent.com/pod-product-compliance
Lightning Source LLC
Chambersburg PA
CBHW031629160426
43196CB00006B/344